Calculators and Cash

Calculators and Cash

Case Studies in Financial Accounting, Audit, and More

Alla Volodina, Marc Colasanti, and Alexandra Popa

CS BUSINESS PRESS
Toronto | Vancouver

Calculators and Cash: Case Studies in Financial Accounting, Audit, and More
Alla Volodina, Marc Colasanti, and Alexandra Popa

First published in 2024 by
Canadian Scholars, an imprint of CSP Books Inc.
180 Bloor Street West, Suite 1401
Toronto, Ontario
M5S 2V6

www.canadianscholars.ca

Library and Archives Canada Cataloguing in Publication

Title: Calculators and cash : case studies in financial accounting, audit, and more / Alla Volodina, Marc Colasanti, and Alexandra Popa.
Names: Volodina, Alla, author. | Colasanti, Marc, author. | Popa, Alexandra, author.
Identifiers: Canadiana (print) 20230564461 | Canadiana (ebook) 2023056447X | ISBN 9781773383903 (softcover) | ISBN 9781773383910 (PDF) | ISBN 9781773383927 (EPUB)
Subjects: LCSH: Accounting—Case studies. | LCGFT: Case studies.
Classification: LCC HF5636 .V65 2024 | DDC 657—dc23

Cover design by Krista Mitchell
Cover image by InspirationGP / iStock
Page layout by S4Carlisle Publishing Services
Printed and bound by CPI Group (UK) Ltd, Croydon, CR0 4YY

EU Authorized Representative: Mare Nostrum Group B.V., Mauritskade 21D, 1091 GC Amsterdam, The Netherlands, gpsr@mare-nostrum.co.uk.

Canadä

CONTENTS

PART ONE

Overview

Introduction

This casebook contains 28 cases covering the full range of financial accounting and audit, tax, and finance topics at the introductory, intermediate, and advanced levels. The cases are intended to supplement the broad study of accounting concepts, to challenge students to develop depth in core competency areas, and facilitate in-class discussions to help students develop critical thinking and problem-solving skills.

PURPOSE AND NATURE OF CASES

Cases outline and emulate real-life business scenarios where the expertise of a Chartered Professional Accountant (CPA) would be required. Each case starts off with a description of a company, the nature of its operations, and a broad problem statement such as, "I need to get audited financial statements for my bank loan." Users of the financial statements (e.g., the bank, an investor, the owners) and their objectives (e.g., assess liquidity/profitability, maximize cash flow, minimize purchase price) will be introduced followed by a variety of company-specific issues referred to as "assessment opportunities."

Students are expected to address these assessment opportunities using the appropriate financial accounting, audit, tax, and/or finance concepts, linking their analysis and recommendations back to the users and objectives. This format encourages students to recognize preparation biases and evaluate the tangible impact of each recommendation, forming the habit of thinking about the "so what?" or "real" implications of day-to-day and one-off business decisions. To illustrate this, we have included the responses to two sample cases, which we encourage readers to review, especially if unfamiliar with accounting cases. A comprehensive solution is provided to both, illustrating how problem-solving and critical thinking skills can be applied. For any specific issue in the case (assessment opportunity), students could receive one of the following rankings:

NC – Nominal Competency
RC – Reaching Competency
C – Competent
CwD – Competent with Distinction

REAL-LIFE APPLICATIONS

The role of a CPA is complex, multi-faceted, and often very dissimilar to the expectations students form of their careers during their undergraduate and post-graduate studies. Theoretically, issues that CPAs are tasked with solving are black and white, having a clear-cut, "correct" course of action. However, in the real world, these issues are often much harder to resolve as CPAs have to take into account budgetary and time constraints, conflicting company–stakeholder priorities, and several other factors.

Real-life questions vary greatly from client to client and industry to industry. That is why it is critical for students to understand and practice how to apply their knowledge. Practicing how to utilize critical thinking skills (using cases such as these) allows students to prepare for actual client demands. Examples of real-life questions that clients could ask in different contexts follow.

Financial Accounting

- We've been developing a new product in-house and have been recording all associated costs on the balance sheet. We're creating an asset for later use after all, but I just wanted to check if we're allowed to do this?
- Customers keep returning a product due to low satisfaction with its utility, which makes me wonder if we have a product defect. If we do, are there any implications on the inventory balance I should be recording?
- A customer just placed a deposit on a future service to be completed. Would this be considered revenue for my company?

Audit

- Stakeholders want to validate that we're operating in an environmentally conscious manner. Our internal accountant suggested we get someone to provide some external assurance on this, but I'm not sure what they mean. How can we do this?
- I need a bank loan and the bank tells me they need to have some confidence in my financial statements. Is that something an auditor can help me with?
- Our company has just implemented a new system for tracking and recording inventory. Can you tell me whether or not our controls are operating effectively?

Tax

- I have been operating my business as a sole proprietorship but heard that I can save on taxes by incorporating. Is this true? Is there anything else I need to consider prior to incorporating?
- My company just hired an individual to help with some of our systems, and they asked to be paid as an independent contractor. Am I able to do this?
- Our family just sold both our primary residence and cottage. Am I able to allocate my principal residence exemption to either property? If so, how should I allocate it?

Finance

- I'd like to expand into a new business line and from my initial assessment it seems to be profitable. Could you take a look at my analysis and provide any feedback?
- When can I expect to break even on this project? As long as it's profitable in three years, I will move forward with it. If there are other factors you think I should consider, can you please prepare a summary of them and relate them back to my corporate strategy?
- I'm looking to purchase a new piece of machinery. Are you able to conduct a discounted cash flow analysis to calculate the expected payback period on my investment?

The cases presented in this casebook are designed to teach aspiring CPAs how to resolve complex client issues, prioritize competing objectives, and simulate the process of offering advice and providing solutions to clients in an engaging and educational way.

After working through this casebook, students should

1. Be able to prepare well-thought-out, accurate, and comprehensive solutions to simulations of real-life client issues.
2. Have a deeper understanding of financial accounting, audit, tax, and finance topics and their real-world implications.
3. Feel better prepared to handle the challenges of being a CPA.
4. Know how to address client concerns while considering different users and their objectives.

SAMPLE CASE 1

Liber Inc.

Erika Dean owns 60% of Liber Inc., a small bookstore chain that specializes in business literature located in a busy city. Her brother, Ralph, owns the other 40%, but has never been actively involved in the business. Liber has been in business for 30 years. Liber's stores are located in lobbies of several downtown skyscrapers. The locations are key to Liber's success.

Erika's son, Harris, who now manages Liber, is paid a straight salary with no bonus. Clarkson Consolidation is a buyout organization that has been purchasing local bookstores to amalgamate this fragmented industry. Erika and her son firmly believe in keeping Liber in the family and they don't want to sell the business. However, Ralph has indicated that Erika should buy out his shares, or he will sell his interest to Clarkson Consolidation.

It is year-end and Harris hired you to review the company's accounting policies and assist in the preparation of the financial statements. Once the statements are finalized, Ralph will show them to Clarkson Consolidation. Erika says, "Given that it is now November 15, 2022, our fiscal year-end is fast approaching. Therefore, I would like you to tell me what accounting policies we will need to adopt when preparing the December 31 financial statements. The statements have never been audited before, and I can imagine that a lot of our current accounting policies are incorrect. We would like to follow accounting standards suitable for private enterprises this year when preparing the statements. Also, please let us know if you have any suggestions on our internal controls." You make some notes (see Exhibit I) from your conversation with Erika and Harris, and realize that all of the accounting issues you noted down will need your attention. You start writing your report with the intent of thoroughly describing the accounting issues involved and providing recommendations.

Harris has already prepared financial statements as of October 31, 2022, using accounting policies that he thought to be correct. He majored in English literature in university and admits he never took an accounting class except for in high school.

EXHIBIT I: EXTRACTS FROM DISCUSSIONS WITH ERIKA DEAN AND HARRIS DEAN

Books

Erika is an avid collector of books and owns a number that have been signed by famous authors. She originally purchased these books when she was just starting the business and had them signed by the authors she met as she became a more prominent figure in the industry. They are for sale and are displayed around one of the downtown stores. Given that the books are no longer in circulation and have been signed by their authors, they are considered "collector's items." Erika estimates they are worth $10,000 each. There are approximately 15 of these highly collectible books in Liber's inventory. The exact price for such books is negotiated between Liber and interested buyers at the time of purchase.

Liber is often asked by small publishing companies to sell their books. However, Harris does not want to risk holding inventory that might not sell. Therefore, he allows the books to be placed in the store but will only pay the publisher for each copy sold. If the inventory does not sell, the books are returned to the publisher with no questions asked. There is approximately $500,000 worth of such inventory in the stores and this has been recorded on the balance sheet. To recognize the inventory, Harris recorded the following journal entry when the books were delivered to the stores: Dr. Inventory, Cr. Cost of Goods Sold.

Normally, bookstores in the area focus on books by North American authors only. Liber gained its popularity by importing books from Europe and keeping a large inventory of European titles in stock. When shipping books from Europe, Liber has to pay shipping costs, taxes, and import duties on the books. All payments except for import duties are made in British pounds and euros, while the import duties are paid to the Canadian government in Canadian dollars. Harris recently received a notification from the Canadian government that Liber had been mistakenly charged an additional $10,000 in import duties and that they would be refunding the money within the next six weeks.

To offset the expensive purchases of European books, Liber receives vendor rebates from European publishers if a certain volume of books is purchased. For example, if Liber purchased more than 15,000 copies of *Parmalat: The European Enron*, a popular book on an accounting fraud case that occurred in Italy, Liber will receive a 10% discount on any copies purchased of that title.

So far this year, Liber has purchased 12,000 copies. Erika says that the book is selling but not as well as she had hoped.

Sales

While the majority of revenue comes from sales to individuals, Liber caught a lucky break when a new but growing Institute of Business Professionals moved into a building next door. The institute offers continuing education classes to adult students, and asked if they could use Liber's store as an "on-campus bookstore." Harris happily agreed as he recognized that this will boost sales significantly. There are two revenue streams associated with the institute: one, the institute purchases bulk orders of books out of its budget and hands them out to its students, and two, it requires students to purchase their individual course texts, which are paid for at the time of purchase.

Last fiscal year, the institute made a large order of $450,000 worth of books for the upcoming semester. At that time, revenue was recognized on the financial statements. Harris and Institute CEO Tianna Barkley are on very good terms but Tianna confidentially told him that the institute is being investigated by the government for alleged fraud. She admits she had no idea about the fraud but says that the employees involved in the fraudulent activities completely drained the institute of cash. Tianna says that despite being fairly young, the institute has a profitable business model and will be able to return to profitability quite soon and restore a healthy cash balance within a year or two. As of today, Liber has not received a payment for the large order of books. Tianna reassured Harris that the institute will be able to make a payment within the next 12 to 16 months.

Liber sells a significant number of gift cards given that business customers are always in a rush and don't have time to look for the right book as a gift. Currently, Liber recognizes revenue for the gift cards when they are purchased. The gift cards do not expire.

Rewards Program

In February 2022, Liber implemented their LiberRewards Loyalty program, which entitles cardholders to receive discounts on their purchases. Each card expires after 12 months. Liber adds a point to the card balance for each two dollars spent at the store every time a purchase is made. Once a customer collects 500 points, they can redeem them for a book up to $20 in value. So far, no customers have redeemed their points. According to Erika, most customers currently have approximately 100 points and only a small percentage have somewhere between 300 to 400 points. No journal entries have been made in relation to the loyalty cards.

Employee Satisfaction

Liber continues to focus on employee satisfaction and maintaining high levels of employee engagement. For example, employees at the head office receive free lunches and coffees, and are regularly invited to contribute their ideas at management forums. These initiatives have been so successful that Liber was recognized by an independent staffing, recruitment, and HR company as the number two employer in the Canadian retail industry. Erika is convinced that because of this ranking (any ranking in the top ten is considered superb), Liber will be able to spend less time and money recruiting new staff. This will also help ensure that only the best staff are recruited in the future. However, management also realizes that building a strong employer brand is an ongoing task that Liber is committed to.

Daily Operations and New Business Opportunities

For better customer service, the stores stay open until 9:00 p.m. throughout the week. The stores are slow between 5:00 p.m. and 9:00 p.m., so a university student is in charge of each store during these hours and closes down the stores on their own. To close the store, the student cleans up and puts the cash register as well as collectible books, if they are being displayed, in a safe.

Erika and Harris are committed to continuously growing their business. They believe their relationship with the Institute of Business Professionals has been very successful and they had an idea to develop business opportunities with other continuing education institutions. The company recently hired a new business development specialist, Marcus Martin. His main responsibilities are to visit different "boutique" educational institutions and promote Liber for all their textbook needs. When Marcus is not on the road, he works from home responding to emails and making calls.

Marcus was given a corporate credit card to use for any business-related expenses, i.e., travel, meals, and entertainment costs, as well as anything related to his home office, i.e., computer, desk, and chairs. Erika and Harris also have corporate credit cards that they use to pay for Liber's operating expenses, including inventory purchases and capital expenditures such as cash registers and shelving units. All of the statements are received on the 15th of each month. Harris immediately pays off the cards in full but does not have the time to review the statements in detail. When the credit card payments are made, Harris records them in the accounting system.

EXHIBIT II: BALANCE SHEET

Liber Inc. Balance Sheet As of October 31, 2022	
Assets	
Current Assets	
Cash	$ 25,000
Accounts receivable - Institute of Business Professionals	450,000
Accounts receivable - other	148,000
Inventory - collectible books	150,000
Inventory - books received from publishers for sale	500,000
Inventory - books	142,000
Employee satisfaction program	248,000
	1,663,000
Property, Plant, and Equipment	1,248,200
	2,911,200
Liabilities	
Current Liabilities	
Bank indebtedness	$ 15,000
Accounts payable	254,800
	269,800
Long-Term Debt (Payable December 31, 2023, 6% annual interest)	450,000
	719,800
Shareholders' Equity	
Common shares	$ 150,000
Retained earnings (deficit)	2,041,400
	2,191,400
	2,911,200

SAMPLE CASE 1 – SAMPLE RESPONSE

Liber Inc.

To: Harris and Erika Dean
From: Advisor, CPA

RE: REVIEW OF LIBER'S ACCOUNTING POLICIES AND PREPARATION OF THE FINANCIAL STATEMENTS

My role is to advise you, Harris, regarding the review of Liber's accounting policies and the adoption of Accounting Standards for Private Enterprises in your fiscal 2022 financial statements. I will also evaluate your internal controls and provide an assessment of any weaknesses. Since you majored in English literature and have not taken an accounting class since high school, I understand that the financial statements you prepared may contain some errors, which I will correct.

USERS OF FINANCIAL STATEMENTS/OBJECTIVES

You, Harris, and your mother, Erika, are interested in the valuation of the business since you want to determine the price of Ralph's shares. You also want to evaluate whether to purchase the shares yourselves or allow Clarkson Consolidation to become a 40% owner of the business. You are both the primary users.

Ralph and Clarkson Consolidation are interested in evaluating Liber's profitability and determining its valuation to determine the share price. They are the secondary users of the financial statements.

The bank is also an important user since Liber has a $450,000 loan repayable at the end of fiscal 2023. The bank is interested in evaluating cash flows to determine if Liber is able to repay the loan plus 6% annual interest. If there are any covenants associated with the loan, such as maximum debt-to-equity or minimum current ratio, the bank would be interested in evaluating whether Liber is in compliance with them. If any assets are being used as collateral for the loan, the bank would be interested in evaluating the assets' value.

PREPARERS OF FINANCIAL STATEMENTS

Harris is currently Liber's active manager. He also prepares the financial statements and has had autonomy over the financial accounting policies since Erika is not actively involved in the daily management or bookkeeping. Harris's goal is to decrease net income, as this will be the basis of the price of Ralph's share buyout.

CONSTRAINTS

Since Liber is a private company, it does not have to comply with ASPE or IFRS. However, since Harris and Erika would like to follow ASPE this year when preparing the statements, I will treat ASPE as a constraint.

ISSUES

Inventory – Value of the Collectible Books

The issue is how to determine what value the collectible books should be recorded at. The books are currently recorded on the balance sheet at $150,000.

Under ASPE, inventory must be recorded at the lower of cost and net realizable value (LCNRV). Erika purchased these books several years ago while they were still in circulation, prior to having been signed by their respective authors, which means that the cost of the books is minimal. Net realizable value is defined as the estimated selling price in the ordinary course of business net of any selling costs. Since these books have been signed by the authors and are no longer in circulation, Erika estimates that each book is worth $10,000, which is significantly more than their original purchase price.

Conclusion: The books cannot be recorded at their estimated selling price of $10,000 and must be written down according to their original purchase price.

This will decrease net income due to a significant inventory write-down, which is in line with Erika and Harris's objective.

Inventory – Treatment of Books Held on Consignment

The issue is that a consignment inventory of $500,000 is currently recorded on the balance sheet. Under ASPE, inventory can only be recorded on the balance sheet if it meets the following asset criteria:

- *Future benefit should be present and should be reasonably measurable.* This criterion is not met since there is no certainty that the books will sell.
- *The entity should be able to control access to the future benefit.* This criterion is not met since the entity has no control over the books, which can be given back to the publishers with "no questions asked" and at no cost or risk if they do not sell.
- *Transaction giving rise to the enterprise's right to the benefit has to occur.* This criterion is not met as Liber is simply displaying the books in the store and will pay the publisher for each copy sold.

Conclusion: Consignment inventory should not be recorded on the books since risks and rewards have not been passed from the seller to Liber. The journal entry recorded is incorrect because it increases inventory (as discussed above) and artificially decreases COGS (since it has been credited). This illustrates that Harris is not a sophisticated preparer of financial statements. The entry needs to be reversed, which will decrease net income (due to the Dr. to Cost of Goods Sold).

Inventory – Purchases and Government Rebates Receivable

The issue associated with the books imported from Europe is multi-faceted.

First, all costs paid in British pounds and euros (i.e., shipping costs and taxes) must be converted to the reporting currency of Canadian dollars when recorded in the trial balances and presented on the financial statements (if this has not already been done). This will increase the cost of inventory since British pounds and euros are worth more than Canadian dollars, which will ultimately decrease net income once the inventory is sold. The import duties are already paid in Canadian dollars, so no currency conversion is needed for these costs.

Second, an accounts receivable (AR) balance should be recorded for the import duties charged by accident and the inventory amount must be reduced by the same amount. The entry will be Dr. Accounts Receivable, Cr. Inventory for $10,000.

Third, there is the issue of the treatment of the vendor rebates that Liber receives from European publishers if a certain volume of books is purchased. The vendor rebates can be accounted for in the inventory if Harris and Erika believe that the book will sell and require a purchase above the 15,000 required threshold. Alternatively, since Liber does not have any prior experience with this title and has no clear indication of whether it will sell, the vendor rebate should not be accounted for in inventory. Since the book has not performed well on shelves so far, it is unlikely that the remaining 3,000 copies required to trigger this rebate will be purchased by Liber and the 10% discount should not be accounted for in inventory.

Accounts Receivable – Write-Off of AR Balance from the Institute of Business Professionals

The issue is whether to discount the recorded accounts receivable at present value, as its collection is expected in 12 to 16 months, or to write the balance off completely.

On the one hand, the institute is a new business that currently has no cash due to the fraudulent activities. This indicates that there is a low chance of collectability and, therefore, the AR should be written off. On the other hand, Tianna says that despite being fairly young, the institute has a profitable business model and will be able to return to profitability quite soon and restore the healthy cash balance within one to two years.

Conclusion: ASPE does not specifically require that accounts receivable be discounted since it is normally a current assets account. Nevertheless, it would make sense to consider the time value of money since the accounts receivable involves a lengthy collection period. When discounting, 6% should be used as the discount rate since Liber has a bank loan with an annual interest rate of 6%.

Revenue Recognition – Gift Cards

The issue is whether revenue from the gift cards should be recorded when purchased. Per ASPE, revenue can be recognized only when all of the following criteria are met:

- *Performance has to be complete (i.e., the seller transfers all the significant risks and rewards to the buyer).* This criterion is not met as the risks and rewards are transferred when the gift card is redeemed rather than at the time of sale.
- *Collectability has to be assured.* This criterion is met because payment has been made upfront in exchange for the gift card, which can be redeemed at a later date.
- *Reasonable assurance has to exist regarding the measurement of the consideration and the extent to which goods are returned.* Revenues are known at the time of sale as the purchase price of the gift card is known; however, the costs associated with the goods returned is unknown until the time of purchase, unless Liber has a consistent gross margin.

Conclusion: Revenue cannot be recorded at the time of sale, as performance has not been achieved. Since gift cards do not expire, they should be recorded as revenue when redeemed. If Liber has data concerning the gift card redemption rate (i.e., breakage rate), they can recognize the percentage of gift cards expected to be collected based on historical percentages. Overall, the treatment of deferring revenue until redemption or reducing revenue recorded based on the breakage rate will decrease net income. This will decrease the purchase price of Ralph's shares, in line with Harris and Erika's objectives.

Liability – Rewards Program

The issue is whether Liber should record a liability for its rewards program. Per ASPE, liability should be recorded if the following criteria are met:

- *The entity will be required to sacrifice some resources to meet its responsibility.* This criterion is met as Liber will have to provide a credit whenever customers redeem points earned towards purchases.
- *The responsibility obligates the enterprise leaving it little or no discretion to avoid it.* This criterion is not met since currently no customer has redeemed points and the program has been active for a year. However, customers who recently activated their cards still have an entire year to redeem their points and may meet the 500-point threshold at this time. As well, it is currently November 15, which gives existing loyalty card holders ~46 days to meet the 500-point threshold.

For customers who have 400 points, this means they need to spend $200 before year-end, which is likely as the winter holidays are coming up, which often drives higher expenditures.
- *The transaction or event obligating the entity has already occurred.* This criterion is met as the customers are earning points with every purchase made.

Conclusion: Based on the above, the liability must be recorded. This is also in line with the principle of conservatism and the concept of matching revenues to expenses (customers purchase books under this rewards program and earn points that they can redeem).

Asset Recognition – Employee Satisfaction Program

The issue is whether the employee satisfaction program should be recognized as an intangible asset on the balance sheet. Per ASPE, an intangible asset can only be recognized if the following criteria are met:

- *Future benefit is probable and will flow to the entity.* As identified by Erika, not as many resources will go into recruiting staff and the best staff will be recruited now that Liber has been recognized as the number-two employer in the Canadian retail industry by an independent staffing, recruitment, and HR company. However, this benefit cannot be measured and therefore this criterion is not met.
- *The cost of the benefit is measurable.* This criterion is met as Liber has paid all expenses (such as free lunches and coffees) associated with the employee satisfaction program.

Conclusion: Based on the above, the intangible asset criteria are not met. In addition, this is not an intangible asset as it is not separable from the entity and it does not arise from contractual or other legal rights. Therefore, these expenses cannot be capitalized and must continue to be expensed, which will have no impact on net income or the purchase price of Ralph's shares.

Internal Controls

Issue: Marcus has been given a credit card and Harris does not review credit card statements.

Implication: Since statements are not reviewed and Marcus's purchases are not approved, Marcus could be spending money on things that Liber might not need or making personal purchases that are flowing through the income statement undetected.

Recommendation: Marcus should be reimbursed for his expenses made with his personal credit card only if Harris approves the expense. This will eliminate any incentive or opportunity for Marcus to submit non-work-related expenses and misuse his position as the new business development specialist.

Issue: A part-time employee who works in the evenings has access to cash in the cash register.

Implication: The employee is in a position to commit and conceal fraud (theft of cash) since there is no requirement for them to count cash at the end of the day and cash to sales is not reconciled.

Recommendation: Have two employees close the store so that they keep each other accountable (this does not eliminate the threat of fraud if the employees collude). Hiring another employee will increase salaries expense and decrease net income, in line with your objectives. In addition to this, it is important to ensure that cash in the cash register is reconciled to sales made during the day and that any discrepancies are followed up on with the store's staff. To make follow-up easier, employees should each have a POS login so that transactions can be traced to the appropriate employee responsible for the cash register during the day.

Accrual Accounting

The issue is that ASPE requires that accrual, rather than cash, accounting is used when recording journal entries and preparing the financial statements. Currently, Harris records expenses when credit card statements arrive. This can result in some expenses being recorded in the wrong period (e.g., expenses that are incurred in fiscal 2022 may be recorded in fiscal 2023, which overstates net income in fiscal 2022). It can also result in the inappropriate expensing of capital assets purchased using credit cards when the correct treatment would be to capitalize and amortize them. Revenue is also recorded on a cash basis and was discussed in the preceding issues.

Conclusion: Accrual accounting must be used to be compliant with ASPE. The director of accounting will have to adjust the entries that were done incorrectly and should keep track of the cumulative impact on net income to appreciate how much the purchase price of Ralph's shares has changed when using accrual instead of cash accounting.

CONCLUSION

Based on the above discussion, it appears that the net income has been misstated. Many of the adjustments quantified above have resulted in lowering net income, in line with your objectives; however, the total impact of the change to net income and share price will be assessed once the aforementioned corrections to net income are made, including the change from cash to accrual accounting.

Finally, while I understand that you would like to keep ownership of Liber within the family, you need to compare the cash on hand and Liber's ability to take on more debt (as determined by the existing bank loan and any associated covenants) to the purchase price of Ralph's shares. If purchasing his shares puts Liber in a highly leveraged and negative cash flow position, I recommend allowing Clarkson Consolidation to purchase Ralph's shares or looking into alternative arrangements such as the following:

1. Convert Ralph's share ownership to a low-interest loan that Liber can payback within the next few years. Ralph may not agree to this, as he seems to want an immediate payout.
2. Find another buyer who is interested in helping manage Liber as an independent bookstore and who is willing to purchase Ralph's shares. This may be an attractive alternative if you do not want pressure from Clarkson Consolidation to amalgamate Liber in the future.
3. Negotiate with Clarkson Consolidation that you will continue managing the business and make all major decisions with Clarkson Consolidation as a silent 40% owner. If you ever change your mind and wish to sell the business in the future, having Clarkson Consolidation on board as a part owner will make a future sale a lot easier.

SAMPLE CASE 2

Match Makers Inc.

Barbara Agassi is the sole shareholder of an employment agency, Match Makers Inc. (MMI). Barbara founded the agency in 2013, at a time when many professionals were changing their careers due to an economic downturn. She saw an opportunity to open an employment agency to provide career counseling as well as help candidates with their job searches. Over the last several years, Barbara has become well-known in the industry and MMI has been growing steadily.

At the beginning of February 2023, Barbara took a year off for maternity leave. Her husband, Tallis Agassi, was unable to take over MMI's daily operations as he runs his own successful web design business. Barbara hired William Ashford on a one-year contract basis to manage MMI in her absence. William has held many senior management roles, including a CFO position with a large food manufacturing company.

Barbara has always concentrated on growing the business using her excellent public relation skills, but has rarely participated in the preparation of financial statements. Company CFO Victoria Bucklin is responsible for maintaining the financial records. Tallis explained to Barbara that he only looks at two figures—net income and cash flow from operations—to assess the profitability of his own company. Barbara decided to take the same approach and emphasized this to William when he assumed his new position. Barbara is now wondering what the difference is between the two figures and whether one figure is better than the other as a measure of the company's success.

It is now January 15, 2024, and Barbara is considering extending her leave for at least another year to spend more time with her two small children. She is impressed with William's performance and is thinking about asking him to manage MMI permanently. The extracts William provided from the 2023 year-end financial statements are presented below. Barbara hired you, CPA, to help her analyze the financial statements, as well as provide advice on a number of other issues related to her company.

Barbara recently learned that it is customary to provide management with bonus compensation based on the company's performance. If William is hired permanently, Barbara would like to implement an incentive structure for him, but she is unsure of what to base it on. Barbara has considered basing the bonus on 5% of cash flow from operations, but she is open to other alternatives.

MMI has a team of 25 highly skilled recruiting specialists responsible for working with existing clients, as well as actively developing new business. Each recruiting specialist is assigned an industry portfolio, focusing on either temporary or permanent work placements. They are paid an annual salary of $65,000 and are entitled to a three-week paid vacation. However, none of the specialists took their vacation during the 2023 fiscal year. If they do not take their vacation in the next year, MMI will have to pay out their vacation pay.

Job candidates post resumés on MMI's website for free and can remove them at any time. Recruiters pay $2,400 for a membership, which gives them one year of access to the MMI resumé portal. Recruiters may access the website as soon as they pay the membership fee. If the website is down for more than two hours at any time during the year, recruiters' access will be extended to compensate for that downtime. As of December 31, 2023, there were approximately 500 resumes posted on the website. William estimates that given today's job market, around 30 of these candidates will be hired. Based on this estimate, William asked Victoria to book the following adjusting journal entry:

Dr. Inventory 210,000
    Cr. Gain on inventory 210,000
To record approximate value of resumé inventory as of December 31, 2023, based on William Ashford's estimate of successful hires and MMI fee for permanent placements.

MMI recently updated the design of its website and expanded its functions with the help of professional web design company Tallis Ltd. (TL) for a fee of $100,000. To keep the site running around the clock, MMI has a computer specifically dedicated to hosting the website. MMI keeps a backup computer in the storage room, in case the primary host computer breaks down and needs to be replaced. Both computers are amortized over five years.

Recruiters contact candidates and invite them for interviews through MMI. All salary negotiations are also done through the company. Recruiters can interview as many candidates as they wish, but on average only about 10 are interviewed before a position is filled. If a recruiter is filling a permanent position, MMI is paid a set fee of $7,000 once a candidate is hired. If the candidate is fired within the three-month probation period, MMI refunds the fee or helps the recruiters fill the position again at no additional cost. If a temporary position is being filled, MMI receives a fee equal to 5% of the negotiated salary throughout the contract's duration. In fiscal 2023, MMI assisted corporate clients to fill 78 permanent and 140 temporary positions.

Due to a recent downturn in the economy, large corporations are less active in hiring new personnel and are instead filling only the most necessary positions. MMI staff continue to try to develop new business and sign new corporate clients on the website, but their efforts are not as successful as in past years. In an average year, about 200 new corporate clients purchase access to MMI's website, whereas only 75 have signed up this past year. William is convinced, however, that the hard work put into further establishing the agency's name will pay off once the economy recovers.

William remains optimistic and believes that, given the current conditions, MMI has done well in the past year. For example, William personally signed a contract with Good Luck Inc. (GLI), a start-up company that ended up recruiting 20 permanent and 15 temporary staff through MMI. In William's opinion, GLI has a unique business model and should be able to expand quickly. For this reason, William postponed collecting the recruiting fees from GLI, agreeing to wait three years for the company to become well-established.

Barbara also mentioned to you that her sister-in-law, Lia Agassi, has just received her business degree and is looking to start her own business. Since Barbara has chosen to take care of her children and has voiced concerns about not being able to return to work full-time, Lia offered to purchase all of her shares in MMI. Lia would be financing the purchase through a bank loan. If the share purchase takes place, the bank and Lia would require audited financial statements. Lia also asked Barbara to base the purchase price on MMI's net assets times a multiplier of five. Barbara is wondering whether the purchase price should be based on some other measure and, more broadly, whether selling the shares is a good idea.

EXHIBIT I: EXTRACTS FROM MMI FINANCIAL STATEMENTS

Match Makers Inc.

Balance Sheet

As of December 31, 2023 (unaudited)

Assets	
Cash	$ 50,000
Accounts receivable	60,000
Prepaid expenses	10,000
Resumé inventory	210,000
Non-current accounts receivable (Good Luck Inc.)	550,000
Website	100,000
Capitalized employee wages	1,625,000
Total Assets	2,605,000
Liabilities	
Bank indebtedness	$ 50,000
Accounts payable	15,000
	65,000
Shareholders' Equity	
Retained earnings	$ 2,440,000
Common stock	100,000
	2,540,000
Total Liabilities and Equity	2,605,000

EXHIBIT I: EXTRACTS FROM MMI FINANCIAL STATEMENTS (CONTINUED)

Match Makers Inc. Statement of Cash Flows For the Year Ending December 31, 2023 (unaudited)	
Cash Flows from Operating Activities	
Net income	$ 1,650,000
Add: Amortization expense	162,500
Less: Accounts receivable	(10,000)
Less: Resumé inventory	(210,000)
Add: Prepaid expenses	110,000
	1,702,500
Cash Flows from Investing Activities	
Accounts receivable from Good Luck Inc.	$ (550,000)
Business development investment (employee wages)	(1,625,000)
Website development	(100,000)
	(2,275,000)
Cash Flows from Financing Activities	
Bank indebtedness	$ 50,000
	50,000
Net Increase (Decrease) in Cash	**(522,500)**
Cash at beginning of period	572,500
Cash at End of Period	**50,000**

SAMPLE CASE 2 - SAMPLE RESPONSE

Match Makers Inc.

To: Barbara Agassi
From: Advisor, CPA

RE: ANALYSIS OF FINANCIAL STATEMENTS AND OTHER ISSUES RAISED BY BARBARA

My role is to advise you, Barbara. I assume you are not familiar with the preparation of financial statements, as you have not been involved in this process before.

USERS OF FINANCIAL STATEMENTS/OBJECTIVES

You, Barbara Agassi, are interested in performance measurement (net income and cash flow from operations). If you decide to go ahead with the sale to Lia Agassi, then you would also be interested in monitoring the net assets. You are the most important user.

Lia wants to see a lower net assets figure, as this would directly decrease the purchase price. She will also evaluate MMI's performance to ensure that it is a profitable business.

PREPARERS OF FINANCIAL STATEMENTS

William Ashford is currently the active manager of MMI. He also prepares the financial statements and seems to have the final word on MMI's financial accounting policies. For example, Victoria booked at least one transaction at his request. William's bias is to increase the net income and cash flow from operations figures, as these are the measures by which he is being evaluated.

CONSTRAINTS

Since MMI is a private company, it does not have to comply with accounting standards. However, the bank and Lia would require GAAP compliant and audited financial statements if the purchase takes place. Therefore, I will treat GAAP as a constraint.

CONFLICT

Your objectives are in direct conflict with William's objectives in this case because while he wants to maximize net income and cash flow from operations, you want to use these figures to "fairly" measure his performance. Both figures can be manipulated if William decides to act on his bias. The cash flow from operations number represents cash generated through the entity's operational activities and net income represents revenues net of expenses incurred by the entity throughout the year. Both figures are directly affected by the financial accounting policies chosen. I would suggest using a mix of qualitative and quantitative measures (including but not limited to the ones already being used) to evaluate the manager's performance.

ISSUES

Revenue Recognition – Website Access Fee

The issue is whether revenue for the new corporate membership fees has been recognized appropriately. Since there is no unearned revenue balance on the balance sheet, I assume that all revenue collected from the membership fees has been recognized in the current year.

Per Accounting Standards for Private Enterprises (ASPE) in Canada, revenue can be recognized only when all of the following criteria are met:

- *Reasonable assurance has to exist regarding the measurement of the consideration and the extent to which goods are returned.* The criterion is met as the membership fee of $2,400 is paid before access is granted.
- *Performance has to be complete (i.e., the seller transfers all the significant risks and rewards to the buyer).* **On the one hand (alternative 1),** this criterion is met as rewards could be considered transferred at the time the recruiter gains access to the website. **On the other hand (alternative 2),** risks may not be transferred such as in the event that the website is down for more than two hours during the one-year period, which forces MMI to "reimburse" the recruiter for the downtime. Based on this argument, the performance criterion is not met.

Therefore, performance is achieved with the passage of time and should be recognized equally over a 12-month period. Carrying out this recommendation will decrease the net income figure.

Revenue Recognition – Permanent and Temporary Position Compensation

The issue is when to recognize the $7,000 fee that relates to the hiring of permanent positions. Based on the revenue recognition criteria listed above, performance is complete once the employee has been chosen and hired. In addition, collectability is assured since recruiters pay a set fee upon hiring. Reasonable assurance, however, might not exist regarding the extent to which new employees will be fired. A provision for "returns" (or people fired) could be based on historical data, which should be available as MMI has been in business for almost 10 years. Conversely, it is possible that the number of people fired will increase due to the changing economic environment. Since there is no indication either way of how MMI candidates and employees are being affected, I conclude that the company can use its historical data to make estimates, which will enable the immediate recognition of all revenue. This impacts the net income figure positively.

Note that revenue related to temporary positions is now recognized with the passage of time (i.e., payments are received throughout the contract period and recognized as revenue simultaneously). This treatment is correct and there is no issue noted.

Resumé Inventory

The issue is whether resumés should be recognized as an asset on the balance sheet.

As per ASPE, an asset can only be recognized if the following three criteria are met:

- *Future benefit should be present and should be reasonably measurable.* Although William makes what appears to be the conservative estimate about the future benefit related to existing resumés (that MMI capitalized just 30 out of 500 candidates), there is no certainty that 30 candidates will be hired. Thus, I conclude this criterion is not met.
- *The entity should be able to control access to the future benefit.* This criterion is not met since the entity has no control over the resumés, which can be withdrawn by candidates at any time.
- *A transaction giving rise to the enterprise's right to the benefit has to occur.* This criterion is not met as candidates did not enter into an agreement of any sort with MMI. Additionally, the access to the website is free for potential employees.

Based on the above, the asset criteria are not met. In addition, this is not an intangible asset as it is not separable from the entity and does not arise from contractual or other legal rights. Therefore, the journal entry booked by Victoria must be reversed. This will decrease the asset base negatively, which will adversely impact your objective of increasing the purchase price.

Liability – Vacation Pay

The issue is whether MMI should record any liability for its vacation pay.

Per ASPE, liability should be recorded if the following criteria are met:

- *The entity will be required to sacrifice some resources to meet its responsibility.* This criterion is met as MMI will have to pay vacation monies whether the employees take their vacations or simply ask for their pay.
- *The responsibility obligates the enterprise, leaving it little or no discretion to avoid it.* This criterion is met as MMI is obligated to its employees based on the employment contract.

- *The transaction or event obligating the entity has already occurred.* This criterion is met as the employees previously earned their vacation pay.

Based on the above, the liability must be recorded. This is also in line with the principle of conservatism and the concept of matching revenues to expenses (vacation pay earned this year).

Asset Recognition/Employee Wages

The issue is whether employee wages represent a period cost or product cost. In other words, we need to consider whether employee wages should be capitalized (the current treatment) or expensed.

Based on the asset criteria listed above, the future benefit likely exists but is not measurable as we cannot be certain when the economy will recover and how the employees' efforts will then pay off. Therefore, we are not able to confirm whether William's assumption is correct, and, in consequence, the future benefit criterion is not met. Furthermore, while the past transaction criterion is met (i.e., employees have already performed the work and have been paid), the control over the future benefit criterion is not met, as we cannot be certain whether the clients will actually use MMI's services.

Based on the above, MMI cannot record this amount on its financial statements and all employee wages have to be expensed, which will negatively impact the net income figure in the amount of $1,625,000.

Accounts Receivable/Revenue – Good Luck Inc.

The issue here is twofold: first, should the recorded accounts receivable be discounted and recorded at present value, as its collection is expected in three years? ASPE does not specifically require that accounts receivable be discounted since it is normally a current assets account. Nevertheless, it would make sense to consider the time value of money, since the accounts receivable involves a lengthy collection period.

Second, should the associated revenue be recorded? It could be argued that recording revenue in this year's income statement is appropriate as performance has been achieved (i.e., employees have been hired) and all of the fees are set and measurable. On the other hand, it could also be argued that revenue needs to be recorded upon collection only. Despite William's predictions, it appears that GLI is a start-up company that might be unable to pay MMI back. The latter argument is stronger and thus $550,000 should not be recognized.

CONCLUSION

Please note that you are MMI's "key success factor" as you are well-known in the industry due to your excellent public relations skills. Since William is a former CFO and his experience lies primarily in the food industry, I doubt that William has been or will be able to fill your shoes.

MMI is influenced by the current economic downturn, and it is critical that it is managed appropriately. Given the fact that the company started up during the previous economic downturn, MMI should be able to withstand the tough times with the right person at the helm.

Based on the above discussion, it appears that the net income and cash flow figures have been overstated. If we take into account the employee wages adjustment, both figures would be decreased by $1,625,000. That means that the revised cash flow from operations will be $77,500 as opposed to $1,702,500. Based on the fact that William has acted on his bias and the performance of the company has deteriorated substantially, I do not recommend hiring William on a full-time basis. It might be a good idea to sell the business to Lia, as it would allow you to spend more time with your children. However, it appears that Lia might lack the necessary expertise to run the business. Perhaps to start, you could sell her 49% of your shares. This will allow her to gain the relevant experience and you would maintain control of the company while working part-time.

Finally, I am concerned about the short-term viability of the company, as William appears to have borrowed cash for MMI's day-to-day operations since the short-term bank loan amount equals the cash amount as reported on the financial statements. I advise you to immediately take over the company's operations.

PART TWO

Financial Accounting Cases

FINANCIAL ACCOUNTING CASE 1

Watering Can Inc.

You, CPA, were just hired as the Director of Accounting at Watering Can Inc. (WCI). Jack and Melanie Parker are WCI's sole owners. The company opened its first flower store on October 1, 2021.

Jack and Melanie initially invested $50,000 into the business. They also obtained from Jack's uncle Sam a $100,000 loan, which has an annual interest rate equal to 5% of net income and is payable on demand. Over the summer, Sam came up with a new business idea: a fishing gear store in cottage country. He notified the Parkers that he might ask for the loan to be paid back if he decides to proceed with the venture. However, he also said that he will not ask for the loan back if its return is better than the expected return on his future business venture. The Parkers decided to approach Small Bank for a $100,000 loan, just in case Sam asks for his loan to be repaid. The bank requested an audit of the 2023 financial statements for the year ending September 30, and made it clear they will require WCI to show a current ratio of 2:1, which WCI will need to maintain if the loan is approved. That is why the Parkers hired you to help sort through the accounting issues. Melanie asks you to prepare a report about any significant accounting issues and other potential problems.

"I heard that having strong internal controls is very important for a start-up business," Melanie says. "Would you be able to highlight our significant internal control weaknesses, if you find any, and provide recommendations?"

"I'm so happy you joined our company," she continues. "My sister runs a cupcake store, Cake-in-a-Cup Inc., and she's trying to come up with a cash flow statement for her business but has no knowledge of accounting. Would you be able to help her out? I'm providing all of the necessary information in Exhibit I. Please prepare a cash flow statement."

SALES

About 50% of WCI customers order in advance for their flower arrangements for special occasions such as weddings, birthdays, and other family functions. Melanie is famous for her impeccable taste in flower creations, and some customers pre-order their arrangements as much as six months in advance. All non-corporate customers are required to pay by cash when placing their order. Melanie makes daily deposits into WCI's bank account. She added up all deposits from October 1, 2022, to September 30, 2023, to arrive at the revenue figure for the year.

NEW CORPORATE SALES

Jack and Melanie are committed to growing WCI's corporate events business; their goal is to be the preferred flower arrangement company for major corporate events in the area. WCI recently hired Charlie Penn, whose main responsibilities are to promote WCI for special occasions.

Charlie was able to secure 20 new corporate accounts in the most recent fiscal year. It is customary in the flower arrangement business to invoice corporate customers after the event and make the payment due 30 days after the event date. WCI has been very successful with several corporate events held in September, which is when people return from their summer vacations and begin hosting such events again. Melanie promptly sent out the invoices and recognized revenue for all 20 events held during the year. Seven event contracts have not yet been paid (three were held back in March and April). Melanie has not made any journal entries in relation to these events, even though she heard about setting up an allowance for doubtful accounts. She says, "I know there are two methods but I didn't know what they are or which to choose, so I left it so I wouldn't mess up the books."

INVENTORY

Inventory management is a critical part of running a flower shop. Melanie orders flowers every week, which arrive Mondays and Thursdays. Melanie believes that it is critical to offer a great variety of flowers in this tough competitive environment. While she has not been tracking which specific flowers are wasted, she has noticed that she ends up throwing out wilted chrysanthemums more than any other flower, even though they are supposed to last the longest—about 20 days after being cut. As of September 30, WCI had 400 fresh chrysanthemums in the store.

WCI's main supplier, A2Z Flowers Inc. (A2Z), provides a great variety of flowers, as well as other supplies such as pots, vases, and baskets used in arrangements. A2Z charges a flat rate of $100 per delivery regardless of the size of the order. WCI has not invested in inventory management software that could help Melanie estimate how many flowers to buy. For now, she does her best to account for sales in both the slow and busy times (such as Valentine's Day and Mother's Day). A delivery can include as little as 50 flowers and two supply items (e.g., pots) and as much as 500 flowers and 50 supply items. When WCI receives an invoice for a delivery, Melanie pays by cheque and expenses the amount on the financial statements.

FINANCING

A Small Bank loans representative told Jack they would charge WCI an interest rate of 12% and would be interested in securing any collateral WCI might have. Jack is proud that a strategic real estate investment he made on behalf of WCI two years ago is paying off. The market value of WCI's store and land is now $470,000, which is much higher than the original price of $250,000. Jack believes this asset will meet the bank's collateral requirement. Jack asked Melanie to increase the value of the property to $470,000 on the balance sheet, so that the bank can appreciate its value.

EXHIBIT I: FINANCIAL INFORMATION PROVIDED BY MELANIE FOR CAKE-IN-A-CUP INC.

Cake-in-a-Cup Inc.
Comparative Balance Sheet
As of December 31, 2022 and 2023

	2023 (in thousands)	2022 (in thousands)
Assets		
Cash	$ 420	360
Accounts receivable	876	900
Short-term investment	480	180
Inventory	900	840
Land	720	720
Property, plant, and equipment (net of amortization)	5,220	3,900
	8,616	6,900
Liabilities		
Accounts payable	$ 336	420
Salaries payable	24	60
Interest payable	60	36
Income tax payable	108	144
Notes payable	0	360
Bonds payable	1,920	1,200
Shareholders' Equity		
Common stock	$ 4,512	3,600
Retained earnings	1,656	1,080
	8,616	6,900

Cake-in-a-Cup Inc. Incomes Statement For the Year Ending December 31, 2023	
Revenues	*(in thousands)*
Sales revenue	$ 4,560
Expenses	
Cost of goods sold	$ 1,560
Salaries expense	540
Depreciation expense	480
Interest expense	144
Loss on sale of land	0
Income tax expense	840
Net income	996

Notes:

1. Cake-in-a-Cup Inc. did not purchase any land during the year.
2. Cake-in-a-Cup Inc. did not dispose of any property, plant, and equipment (PPE) during the year.
3. For 2022, beginning amortization for PPE was 900 and ending accumulated amortization was 1,380.

FINANCIAL ACCOUNTING CASE 2

MoveIt Inc.

Brothers Sam and Seb Novale established MoveIt Inc. (MoveIt or MII) in March 2022. MoveIt specializes in interior demolition. A typical customer might be a coffee shop or similar business who is moving into a facility that requires removing existing built-in fixtures to make way for new ones. This year, the brothers are applying for a bank loan and need to provide audited financial statements for fiscal 2023, which ended on March 31, 2023. A bank representative promised Sam and Seb that once the financial statements are received and the loan application form is completed, MoveIt will be able to borrow at prime plus 4% (at the moment, prime is 2%). You, CPA, have been hired as a controller. Your first task is to help MII establish accounting policies for some of the complex transactions that took place during the year. MII is planning to go public as soon as possible.

The brothers started the company after learning that another demolition company, Complete Demolition Inc. (CDI), was closing. CDI was owned by a family friend who was forced to retire for health reasons. At the time, CDI was unable to fulfill its contractual obligations to two clients. MoveIt purchased one of the contracts in April 2022 and the other in March 2023. While the latter has not yet been fulfilled, the former was a demolition of a coffee shop's interior in advance of it being renovated. Several months after the demolition was complete, the client contracted MoveIt to renovate the remaining eight locations of their coffee shop chain. MoveIt's former bookkeeper suggested keeping one of the purchased contracts on the balance sheet while expensing the other.

Given successful purchase of the contracts, they decided to grow their business by purchasing contracts from other companies going into liquidation or closing down. The brothers already hired an agent on commission tasked with searching for similar opportunities. They are expecting many more transactions involving the purchase of contracts in the upcoming year. This time around, they will also need to pay a 5% commission to the agent.

Interior demolition is a capital-intensive industry. Lacking start-up capital, the brothers decided to rent most of their equipment on an as-needed basis (i.e., depending on the requirements of each contract). MII paid a rental company, KUI Inc., $6,000 to rent equipment such as garbage and hazardous waste disposal bins, floor stripping machines, and other specialized tools. The rental agreement is for three years with an option to extend for two more years. If the garbage bins were purchased instead of rented, they would cost about $5,500, the floor stripping machinery about $3,000, and the remaining smaller tools less than $2,000.

MII also leased a heavy truck that would have cost $30,000 to purchase for $700 per month from another rental company. The lease period is for three years. If the business takes off, MII has an option to renew the lease for another two years for the same monthly fee. The lease allows for the truck to be driven 30,000 kms per year. If they use it beyond the 30,000 kms allotted, MII will be charged an additional fee of $3,000 per year. If the business has some cash available at the end of the three-year lease period, the brothers have an option to purchase the truck for $10,000 or for $5,000 at the end of the five-year lease period. They would prefer to purchase the truck, as they think that purchasing versus renting is more financially sensible.

MII offers its customers interior demolition services at $100 per square foot, including garbage removal. They guarantee complete demolition of a facility within four weeks from the point of signing a contract for properties up to 4,000 square feet. Previous contracts have ranged from as short as one day and as long as 20 days. When either Sam or Seb provide an estimate, they set a specific date of completion. If the deadline is not met, the contract stipulates that MoveIt will reduce its fee by 5% of the total price for each day the project is late. Customers are invoiced within seven days of project completion and payments are due within seven days of receiving an invoice.

Towards the end of the fiscal year, MII's strategy was bearing fruit and the company was rapidly growing its operations. The brothers felt it was time to rent out a small office. To find an office to lease, MII contracted a real estate agent who charged 2.5% on all the lease payments, payable during the period of the lease. The agent found an appropriate office and a lease agreement was signed for three years (with an option to renew for two more years). The lease can be terminated within the three-year period but MII would be required to pay a termination penalty. MII had to carry out some minor renovations (approximately $30,000) to ensure the space was suitable for their needs. The lease payments are $4,000 per month. The building in which the office space is located is fairly new and is expected to last approximately 40 years. If the same level of growth is sustained for the next three years, MII will need to hire more administrative staff and will also need to purchase tools and equipment, as continuing to rent them out will no longer be economical. In this scenario, MII would also need to move into a new office space.

FINANCIAL ACCOUNTING CASE 3

Fun4Kids Inc.

FestiPrêt SA (FPS) is a large, private corporation owned and operated by Annemarie and Jacques Petite. FPS was established in northern France in 1985. The company specializes in mail-in party supplies, such as plastic tableware, balloons, and other decorations.

It is now February 9, 2023. FPS is considering expanding abroad. Annemarie has identified a Canadian company, Fun4Kids Inc. (FKI), as a potential buyout target. FPS hired you, CPA, to further assess these investments.

The financial statements of FKI have never been audited. The company's year-end is December 31, 2022. Annemarie has asked you to prepare a report highlighting any important accounting issues. She intends to request audited financial statements, but she would like your opinion on any significant issues pertaining to the inventory account. FKI does not have any other significant assets, as the rest of the assets are leased and not owned by the company.

Fun4Kids Inc. was established two years ago by Martha Carter. Though FKI has reported positive net incomes in both years, Martha is looking to sell the company so she can spend more time with her four children. The bookkeeping is done by Martha's cousin who does not have formal accounting training. Martha agreed to base the purchase price of the business on its 2022 net assets multiplied by five. The reported net income is $600,000.

FKI manufactures several lines of party supplies. All of the inventory currently held on hand by FKI is listed below.

Inventory	Total cost as of January 1, 2022
Barbie party supplies	$210,000
Hello Kitty party supplies	300,000
Cinderella party supplies	50,000
Teddy Bear party supplies	270,000
Spiderman party supplies	24,000

In June 2022, the Barbie brand was tarnished by a highly publicized campaign. One consequence of this was that customers stopped ordering Barbie products from FKI. As a result, the company wrote off its entire Barbie inventory at that time. By the end of December 2022 though, the manufacturer of Barbie products successfully re-established customer confidence by releasing a new line—"Barbie the Professor." FKI is planning to start manufacturing the line soon since the company has seen a gradual increase in the demand for Barbie-themed party supplies.

FKI employs 10 administrative employees and 10 factory workers. FKI uses the first-in, first-out (FIFO) method to account for its inventory.

FKI produced approximately 800,000 units of party supplies in 2021 and 500,000 units in 2022 (e.g., each plate or cutlery set would count as a unit). Each unit costs approximately $0.95 to produce and sells for $2.00. The company has established a solid relationship with its major supplier and is able to negotiate significant volume discounts. One of the deals guarantees FKI a volume discount of 10% or 20% if FKI purchases enough materials in fiscal 2022 (10% is discounted for producing at least 400,000, and 20% is discounted for more than 550,000 units of party supplies). The materials can be returned for up to six months if not used. FKI receives the rebate when the return period lapses.

Currently, the cost of inventory reported on the financial statements includes all of the building's heat and electricity costs of $50,000, factory staff wages and administrative personnel wages of $100,000, and gross material costs of $325,000.

One of FKI's distinguishing features is the company's 24-hour delivery service guarantee. The company hires drivers on a contract basis across the region. All drivers are required to keep at least 500 units of inventory at home. When a customer makes an order online, FKI processes the order and sends the request to the appropriate driver, depending on the customer's location. The driver is responsible for picking the right amount and type of inventory from his "home stock" and delivering it to the customer. Customers usually pay by cheque or cash (plus any tips) for products delivered.

When inventory levels decrease below the threshold of 500 units, the driver simply notifies management and picks up additional inventory from the head office to replenish their home stock. Drivers drop off payments collected from customers, as well as return any slow-moving units, when they stop by head office to pick up new inventory.

In 2022, FKI began producing handmade statuettes of Cinderella and Spiderman. These are intended to be collectible and one-of-a-kind pieces, as FKI would like to sell them at a high margin. At the beginning of the year, Martha hired a talented sculptor to handmake the first 20 Cinderella and 10 Spiderman statuettes. The sculptor insists on purchasing raw materials that are available only in remote parts of the world. The prices for raw materials fluctuated significantly during the year, from $100 per piece to $1,700 per piece, depending on the availability of the material on the market.

The sculptor makes monthly trips abroad to purchase raw materials such as clay and makes all his purchases in cash. He explained to Martha that he usually buys more materials than are required, as sometimes he simply throws out a piece if he is unhappy with his artistic performance. He submits an annual expense report, as shown below, and FKI reimburses him in full and records the cost on the statement of financial position, and later includes it in the cost of goods sold line item on the statement of profit and loss.

Here is the total expense listing provided by the sculptor for the past year:

Type of expense for fiscal year ending December 31, 2022	**Amount**
Materials used in 20 Cinderella and 10 Spiderman statuettes	$150,000
Other materials (scrap)	50,000
Taxes paid abroad on all materials	30,000
Airfare fees + hotel fees	50,000
Hourly compensation (4,380 hours @ $20)	87,600
Total	**$367,600**

FINANCIAL ACCOUNTING CASE 4

Numbers and Formulas Inc.

Numbers and Formulas Inc. (NFI) is a private company held equally by 10 close friends. However, NFI follows accounting standards suitable for public companies. NFI manufactures no-name brand calculators and currently supplies them to retailers in the region, primarily catering to elementary and high school markets. NFI's primary strategy is to sign long-term contracts with private schools.

NFI is managed by Bill Gill, who has been the company's CEO for six years, with a compensation package that includes a bonus based on net income. Bill advised the owners that the time had come to find a new lender to help finance the company's growth. The owners asked a mutual friend, Brandon Dias, to lend the company $1,000,000 payable in five years.

Brandon is a variety store owner who has never held another corporation's debt security. It is now July 15, 2023, and Brandon has hired you to review NFI's accounting policies. NFI's year-end is June 30. Brandon pays close attention to cash flows in his own business and he has requested a copy of NFI's cash flow statement (see Exhibit I). He was happy to see that NFI's cash position has improved over the last year, but he would still like your opinion about this. He has stated that he is specifically interested in the impact of NFI's new project on the company's cash flow position, current ratio, and debt-to-equity ratio.

NFI has never had its financial statements audited but will do so this year to meet Brandon's request. Currently, the financial statements are compiled by the company's office manager. At present, the company's current debt-to-equity ratio is just over 3:1. This was a significant increase from last year when it was just below 1:1.

NFI has recently developed a new business line, a no-name portable tablet called Learn&Play3000, which is sold for $500 per unit. NFI's owners are excited about this new product. The company was able to sign several contracts with local private schools and delivered over 300 tablets to five schools before June 30. NFI recognized revenue at the time of delivery. The schools have agreed to purchase Learn&Play3000 devices and distribute them to all their students for the upcoming school year. The cost of the devices will be embedded in the tuition fees, so the schools will have no issue financing such a large expense. However, the partner schools explained that they will only be able to pay NFI for the units delivered at the end of October when all of the tuition fees are collected. NFI has agreed to these terms.

The company is vigorously preparing for the new school year, manufacturing approximately 2,000 units of the Learn&Play3000 devices to meet the expected demand over the summer. It costs $250 to manufacture each device.

To prepare for growth in its business lines, at the beginning of the 2023 fiscal year the company purchased a $750,000 facility in the city. The building is depreciated over 80 years on a straight-line basis. The company sold its old building at a gain of $450,000, which has been included in the revenue line on the income statement.

NFI had to borrow some funds from the bank at a 10% interest rate to finance its business growth. This is a relatively higher rate due to the fact that the company is highly leveraged.

EXHIBIT I: STATEMENT OF CASH FLOWS

Numbers and Formulas Inc.
Statement of Cash Flows
For the Year Ending June 30, 2023 (unaudited)

Cash provided by (used in)	
Cash Flow from Operations	
Net loss	-$95,368
Add: amortization expense	785,625
Less: gain on sale of land and building	-350,000
Less: increase in inventory	-495,750
Less: increase in accounts receivable	-185,000
Add: increase in accounts payable	359,086
Add: decrease in prepaid expenses	5,814
	24,407
Cash Flow from Financing Activities	
Increase in long-term debt	$750,000
Increase in bank indebtedness	30,000
	780,000
Cash Flow from Investing Activities	
Purchase of land and building	-$750,000
Sale of land and building	450,000
Sale of private jet	150,000
Moving costs related to manufacturing equipment	-250,000
	-400,000
Increase/(decrease) in cash balance	404,407
Cash balance at the beginning of the year	25,000
Cash balance at the end of the year	429,407

FINANCIAL ACCOUNTING CASE 5

Protein-Way Inc.

Protein-Way Inc. (PW or the Company) is a private company in the meat-packing industry. Five brothers have an equal 20% ownership interest in the company. PW was started in 2015 by one of the brothers, Earl Bens. Five years later, Earl's four brothers were brought into the company as passive investors.

A couple of months ago, Earl's wife filed for divorce after 26 years of marriage. The judge has decided that Earl's wife is to receive the equivalent of 50% of Earl's share in the business. Since Earl's wife is not interested in having a share in the business, Earl has to pay out an equivalent of the share to her. The judge did not specify how the value should be calculated, but he did suggest that it should be based on a multiple of five of the most recent fiscal year's net income. PW's gross revenue for the most recent year is $500,000 and net income is $100,000. PW follows accounting standards suitable for private enterprises.

It is now December 31, 2023, one month after the year-end. You, CPA, are a sole practitioner and you just had your first meeting with Earl. PW had previously used an accounting firm owned by a friend of Earl's wife, so this year he chose your firm instead to prepare the financial statements in accordance with accounting standards suitable for private enterprises. An independent auditor will be appointed by the judge at a later date. Earl would like your opinion about several changes in accounting policies pertaining to current assets. One of Earl's brothers is also concerned about the company's internal controls and Earl would like you to look into this as well.

Below are the notes that you prepared based on your meeting with Earl.

- PW has very little debt and its cost of borrowing is 5%. The bank financed the purchase of some new equipment this fiscal year, and placed a current ratio covenant of 1:1.
- The past year was a bad one for the Canadian meat industry and several PW customers are struggling with financial problems. Even though all of the company's sales are on credit, PW had previously never provided a bad debts provision since their accountant, Erin Badbooks, is not sure how to estimate uncollectible receivables. Until now, she wrote off uncollectible accounts receivable directly whenever she felt the account was no longer collectible. Over the years, she noticed that approximately 5% of sales are ultimately uncollected. Earl contends that while 30% of the receivables 61–90 days old are not collected, 50% of the receivables older than 90 days are not collected, while the rest of the receivables are 98% collected. Earl has asked you to help Erin establish an appropriate policy. However, this year he suggested recording a general provision of $70,000. You have asked Earl to provide you with the aging schedule (see Exhibit I).
- One of PW's longtime customers is Beef Lovers (BL), owned by Joey Lucino. BL is a small but profitable grocery chain that owes PW $40,000. The balance has been outstanding for 180 days, so PW agreed to restructure the receivable. BL has agreed to pay the entire amount in equal installments over the next five years. Earl is considering whether to write down the receivable by 50% since he believes that Joey is sometimes irresponsible.

To better understand internal control issues, you also spent a couple of hours observing PW's day-to-day operations. A shoe box labelled "petty cash" is kept beside one of the printers in the company's accounting department. Accounting staff are instructed to use the cash for any emergencies such as buying a new cartridge, paper towels for the staff kitchen, or mineral water for the main boardroom. Staff are instructed to write down on the box the date, reason for use, and amount of cash that was taken out.

All staff laptops and computer systems, including the accounting software, have a standardized password—"Meat Eater" (the username is also standard—"delicious meat"). The password is intended to protect the company's data in case a laptop is lost or stolen. Erin is responsible for collecting any outstanding AR balances. Her responsibilities include collecting cash or cheques from retailers, making cash deposits into the company's bank account, and updating retailers' outstanding account balances.

Earl regularly monitors stock levels by inspecting the storage facility and estimating whether additional orders for raw materials need to be made. He compiles a list of the required materials and their quantities and gives it to Erin who is responsible for preparing the official purchase orders and sending them to suppliers. All shipments are sent to Erin's attention. When the shipment arrives, Erin matches the purchase order to the shipment to ensure that all goods have been received.

EXHIBIT I: ACCOUNTS RECEIVABLE AGING SUMMARY

Protein-Way Inc.

A/R Aging Summary

As of December 31, 2023

	Current	1–30	31–60	61–90	>90	Total
All You Can Eat Inc.	$ 1,500.00	-	-	-	-	1,500.00
Anything for Breakfast LLP	1,350.00	-	1,350.00	1,350.00	1,350.00	5,400.00
Beef Lovers Inc.	-	-	-	-	40,000.00	40,000.00
Dinner for Two Ltd.	450.00	450.00	450.00	-	-	1,350.00
Food R Us Ltd.	5,000.00	-	-	-	-	5,000.00
Linda Bens	-	-	-	-	3,500.00	3,500.00
Love it and Eat it LLP	4,500.00	-	-	-	-	4,500.00
Love Your Sandwich Inc.	15,000.00	8,000.00	-	-	-	23,000.00
Maple Stores Ltd.	7,500.00	500.00	-	-	-	8,000.00
Meats and Meals Inc.	-	-	-	-	12,000.00	12,000.00
Walter Bens	-	-	-	-	10,000.00	10,000.00
What's Cooking Ltd.	150.00	-	150.00	-	-	300.00
Yummy Sausages Inc.	2,500.00	-	500.00	-	-	3,000.00

FINANCIAL ACCOUNTING CASE 6

Forever&After Inc.

Karen and Michael Cuentos wanted to be part of the wedding planning industry ever since they got married. To that end, the Cuentos incorporated Forever&After Inc. (FAI) five years ago. Their dream was to purchase a plot of land in the city's suburbs and build a banquet hall, but they were unable to find a good deal at the time. Therefore, on April 1, 2018, FAI purchased a small banquet hall in the city, the Paradise Event Centre, for $200,000.

Today is April 26, 2023. The Cuentos have engaged you, CPA, as an independent consultant to advise them on FAI's financial statements. To this point, Karen has done all of the bookkeeping, using financial accounting software. This year, however, you will be responsible for booking all of the major transactions. You have opened your notes to review the timeline of events related to FAI's 2023 fiscal year. FAI's financial year-end is March 31. FAI currently has an outstanding bank loan of $75,000 at a 5% interest rate. The Cuentos also reminded you that the bank placed a current ratio covenant of 1:1 at the beginning of the year. The Cuentos also would like FAI to maintain the return on assets ratio at 5% or higher, in case any future financing is required. The owners hope to one day take FAI public.

Even though business at the Paradise Event Centre had been going along steadily, the Cuentos continued to look for bargain deals on empty plots of land. On April 2, 2022, FAI purchased a 20-hectare parcel of land for $1,500,000. The Cuentos hired contractors for $350,000 to clear the land of trees and prepare a section of the land, approximately 10 hectares, for construction.

The Cuentos hired a construction company to build a banquet hall called the Luxury Escape. Only 10 hectares were used to build the facility. The rest of the land is currently not used.

The Cuentos are not sure what they are going to do with the rest of the land, but Michael heard from a friend that holding and selling it at a premium price in a couple of years might be a good business idea. Michael was very impressed when his real estate agent told him that the land value in the area had increased by 45% by March 2023. He is now considering whether FAI should get more involved with investing in real estate, i.e., purchasing land parcels, holding them, and then selling them at a premium after several years. Michael is wondering if it is possible to show the true value of the land on the financial statements since he is sure all users of the financial statements would be quite impressed.

FAI's main marketing strategy at the Luxury Escape is "Luxury in the middle of nowhere." Karen decorated the banquet hall with a special emphasis on modern style. She plans to keep the place as modern looking as possible, which means replacing the decor and furniture fairly often. She purchased some luxurious but trendy furniture pieces for $900,000. Karen believes the furniture goes out of style every five years or so and is confident that she can resell it for $200,000 after 5 years of use. Michael says the furniture will last approximately 15 years and can be donated afterwards to a local charity. At that point, the fair value would be immaterial.

FAI owns an extensive collection of high-quality linens such as tablecloths, chair covers, and napkins. In 2018, FAI purchased its linen collection from Fancy Linens Inc. for $300,000, which is currently amortized over 20 years. Couples who book their weddings at the Luxury Escape can also rent linens for an additional charge. A representative from Fancy Linens contacted FAI in March 2023 with a recommendation to replace their collection for a total of $150,000. He explained that raw materials significantly decreased in price over the last couple years, which has caused the price of linens to drop. The representative offered to buy back the old collection for $50,000. Karen decided instead that it would be a great idea to buy a new collection for the Luxury Escape but keep the old collection as well and rent it out as a cheaper option. The rental fee for linens is $2,000 per night from the new collection and $1,000 per night for the old collection. Karen estimates that over the next five years, the old linens will be rented out approximately 30 times per year.

In October 2022, the Cuentos were approached by an elderly couple, Mr. and Mrs. Nice, who owned a small hotel across from FAI's newly built wedding venue. Since the couple was about to retire, they offered to sell their hotel to FAI for $500,000. The Cuentos heard many good comments about the hotel from other residents in the area. Plus, they thought it would be a great idea to have a hotel close to the banquet hall so that guests could have the convenience of staying overnight after a big event. FAI obtained ownership of the hotel on December 1, 2022. However, the Cuentos were curious to see whether they made a good deal and invited an expert to give them an appraisal of their purchase. The expert's report states that the land is worth approximately $260,000 to $350,000, and the building is worth no more than $100,000 as it is expected to remain useful for just another 10 years or so.

FINANCIAL ACCOUNTING CASE 7

Overalls Inc.

You, CPA, are a newly hired senior manager of financial reporting with Overalls Inc. (OI), a company that specializes in manufacturing home appliances such as fridges, ovens, and dishwashers.

It is now January 5, 2023, and OI is about to sign an exclusive 5-year supply agreement with Luxury Living Inc. (LLI), a construction company specializing in building high-end homes. The exclusive contract with LLI is the first of its kind for OI. Traditionally, OI has distributed its products through 200 independently owned and operated, non-franchised dealers. Since LLI would be highly dependent on OI if the contract is signed, LLI requested OI's most recent financial statements. You are responsible for finalizing the financial statements for the current year, which just ended on December 31, 2022. OI has a loan of $3,000,000 outstanding from a private investor. The interest rate on the loan is 5%. OI follows accounting standards suitable for private enterprises.

DEALERS

It is up to each OI dealer to decide which inventory to carry and when to replenish their inventories. All dealers submit their orders to the OI head office. If the product is not available, OI will manufacture it in one of their facilities within 30 days. Sales to dealers are recognized as revenue when the order is placed. Before the product is shipped, the dealer is required to make a 50% partial payment in cash, cheque, or credit card. When the product is sold to the end customer, the dealer is to remit the remaining amount. Once the products are received by the dealer, they cannot be returned to OI for refund.

OI's accounting clerk, Mariana Blue, is responsible for collecting payment from the dealers. Accounts receivable are usually collected on time except for dealers who experience special business circumstances such as poor cash flows or unstable financial positions. Mariana noted that over the past fiscal year the accounts receivable turnover ratio had decreased.

OWNED AND LEASED FACILITIES

OI has four manufacturing facilities which are summarized below:

Factory	Location	Facility Leased or Owned	Name of Lessor	Lease Term	Asset's Life	Annual Lease Payment
Factory A	Canada	Leased	Lease-for-You Inc.	40 years	55 years	$100,000
Factory B	France	Leased	Lease-for-You Inc.	10 years	40 years	$125,000
Factory C	China	Owned	N/A	N/A	40 years	N/A
Factory D	Mexico	Owned	N/A	N/A	10 years	N/A

OI has a strong relationship with Lease-for-You Inc. (LFY) and is one of the company's major customers. LFY has just constructed a manufacturing facility in France, costing approximately $1,000,000, which is equivalent to the fair market value of the building, meeting OI's specifications. The Chinese and Mexican facilities were also originally owned and constructed by LFY. The Chinese facility is currently amortized over 40 years. The Mexican facility is no longer amortized as it is not expected to generate any revenue. In 2020, the facility was designated for use in product repairs only while all production activities were shifted to other facilities.

Only the Chinese and Mexican facilities are recorded on the balance sheet for $685,000 and $500,000 respectively.

LAWSUIT

A former dealer is suing OI for $10 million for wrongful termination of his dealer licensing agreement. Legal counsel has confirmed that the claim is without merit but recommended settling for $250,000 to avoid further legal costs and bad publicity.

WARRANTY REPAIRS

One of the strengths of OI's service is its lifelong commitment to fix any equipment it has ever sold, free of charge. When suppliers discontinue unique parts that OI might need for repairs, OI purchases them in bulk and stores them at the Mexican facility.

Two days ago, you read in a national newspaper that an oven manufactured by OI unexpectedly blew up in a customer's home, significantly damaging the building. The customer is not expected to file a lawsuit as OI promptly contacted the customer and offered to pay for all the damages. However, management is uncertain as to which facility produced the oven, but is committed to testing the most popular oven models to ensure that the problem is isolated.

BONDS

OI has recently issued bonds for $5 million to a private investor. The bonds pay 4% annually for the next 10 years until their maturity date. OI required these funds for its expansion into the booming Brazilian market. Even though interest payments will commence in 2024 on a retroactive basis, OI is required to not exceed the debt-to-equity ratio of 2:1. If the covenant is breached, the bonds become convertible.

PART THREE

Intermediate Financial Accounting Cases

INTERMEDIATE FINANCIAL ACCOUNTING CASE 1

PicDepot Inc.

PART 1

Halley and Brian Hammond are owners and founders of PicDepot Inc. (PDI). Halley is an accountant by training but has not worked in the field since 1985, when she quit her job to open a photography studio. Her business steadily grew, causing Halley's husband, Brian, to leave his full-time job in IT to help her.

Today, PDI is a profitable private internet-based company, offering commercial digital imagery, such as licensed photographs and illustrations. Individuals and companies can use the imagery for their websites, marketing materials, publications, and books. Any approved contributor can upload digital content to the PDI-operated website. In return, the contributor receives a royalty payment every time the image or illustration is downloaded by a client.

Halley and Brian are both extremely dedicated to the business. They are confident that PDI will grow further and eventually go public. For now, Halley and Brian approached Lilly Bruce with a proposal to invest in PDI. The Hammonds were looking for a debt investor and met Lilly through a family friend. While Lilly travels frequently to Canada, she lives overseas, managing an international family business with her brother. Lilly was intrigued by the idea of investing in PDI, but due to time constraints and an unfamiliarity with accounting standards (which PDI currently uses), she is presently unable to review the financial statements carefully.

Today is December 13, 2023, and PDI's year-end is November 30. Lilly hired you, CPA, to advise her on this investment opportunity. She provided you extracts regarding the investment from a presentation the Hammonds gave her on December 10 (Exhibit I) and her notes from the meeting (Exhibit II). She asked you to prepare a report: "Please clarify how accounting rules work in relation to any significant accounting issues pertaining to PDI? I'm only interested in the statements for the fiscal year that just ended (Exhibit III), as the financial statements have yet to be audited. I have the audited financial statements for the five years prior to 2023. PDI follows accounting standards suitable for public enterprises. I'm pretty sure PDI's financial statements are in order, yet they have not been audited. So if PDI booked something that should not have been booked or vice versa, I would like to know. Also, let me know what you think of PDI as an investment in general."

EXHIBIT I: EXTRACTS FROM THE PRESENTATION PRESENTED TO LILLY BRUCE BY PDI

Overview – Financing Required and Uses

- Need $500,000 in debt financing but currently completely debt-free
- Terms negotiable; proposed terms – loan payable in 2030, 5% annually
- If cannot agree on terms, possible alternative to debt financing is 10,000 PDI shares for $50 per share
- Uses of financing:
  - Purchase of new computers and other capital assets
  - Investments in newly developed software to enhance customer experience on our website
  - Enhance marketing and advertising to grow PDI's customer base
  - Purchase real estate to use as PDI's permanent headquarters
  - Payout dividends to shareholders

Compare Our Performance to Competitors

- Profit Margin Ratio = Net income / (Sales x 100%)
  - PDI (2023 fiscal): 4,269,329 / (15,890,980 x 100%) = 27%
  - Our competitors: 20–25%
- Debt to Equity
  - PDI (2023 fiscal): No loans = no debt!
  - Our competitors: average of 2:1
- Return on Assets = Net income / Average total assets
  - PDI (2023 fiscal): 4,269,329 / (26,270,990 + 15,389,000) = 10%
  - Our competitors: 10–30%

EXHIBIT II: NOTES MADE BY LILLY BRUCE DURING THE PDI PRESENTATION

Users/Subscribers

PDI clients can pay for either monthly or yearly access to the database, allowing them to download a limited number of images each day for the duration of their subscription (for example, 50 images per day). The subscription option was introduced in fiscal 2023.

If customers choose not to subscribe to either access plan (e.g., for users who need fewer images), there is an option to purchase individual images for a set price of $7. If a customer downloads 10 images, but did not subscribe to the monthly or yearly access, they may download one image for free. Since the promotion came into effect at the beginning of the 2023 fiscal year, 20,000 free images were downloaded. To access the free download, a client must first accumulate enough credits and then explicitly select "redeem free picture." If this selection is not made, the user's credit card on file will be automatically charged.

Customers must pay using their credit card before images can be downloaded. PDI recognizes all payments when received from customers under the "sales" line item on the income statement. In 2023, to offset slow business during the fourth quarter of the fiscal year, the company also introduced several promotional discounts (e.g., 15% on imagery purchased).

Contributors

Anyone wanting to contribute to PDI's website must provide samples of his/her work to the company for quality control. If the samples are acceptable, the uploader is granted "approved contributor" status, signs a standard agreement with PDI, and is provided an individual username and password. The contributor can then upload their images and illustrations at any point in time. Contributors must obtain the written consent of any models depicted in their images.

Contributors receive a royalty fee of $1 each time an image of theirs is downloaded. A single photo may be downloaded by multiple users. All photos are automatically purged by PDI's software five years from the date of posting or can be removed from the website by the contributor (contributors retain their copyright at all times). An administrative clerk tracks and records all downloads in bi-yearly reports (on December 31 and July 1), which ensures additional efficiency in operations. The summary reports are then sent to the accounting department for payment, which is made almost immediately and a "Cost of Sales – Contributor Royalties" account is adjusted for the payment made.

Company Operations

PDI had to find a new home after it outgrew its original space, moving into its new premises, conveniently located close to the Hammonds' home, at the beginning of fiscal 2023. PDI occupies two floors in the building. The building's remaining lifespan is projected at 25 years. Lease payments are pretty steep—$10,000 per month per floor—as this is a very popular area. Halley and Brian initially wanted to purchase the two floors of the building for the asking price of $750,000, but decided against laying out so much cash up front. They ended up signing a three-year lease this year with a one-year optional renewal period. It was a good decision not to purchase the building, as they discovered that the local government will be appropriating the land and building within five years, to make way for a public transit expansion.

Company Innovations

In today's competitive environment, the Hammonds believe in investing in continuous improvement. At the outset of the fiscal year, the owners decided that it was time to upgrade their website. At that point, the image library contained over 15,000,000 pictures. It was critical to ensure that the search engines built into the website were efficient, allowing customers to easily find the right imagery. An "innovation" team was put together, consisting of four IT specialists and one graphic designer. The salaries of these professionals add up to $1,160,000 annually. The team spent one month researching current products, hoping to use existing technologies for the new website, but soon realized that they would need to build it entirely from scratch. The IT specialists were eager to develop an exclusive search mechanism that would be PDI's pride and joy. In early May, the team entered the testing phase. Within two weeks, it became evident that the new search engine provided virtually the same results as the old search engine. There was no increased efficiency. The team went back to the drawing board and presented another version of the search engine in September. The management was pleased with the new website, noting only a few minor "bugs" and necessary corrections. Management stated, "If everything goes according to plan, the website should be up and running on January 2, 2024."

Management also asked the team to develop a new website homepage to serve as a quick PDI introduction. The site had to include commonly found pages such as "About Us," "Why PicDepot is Best," and "Testimonials." The team took four weeks out of their busy schedules in 2023 to complete the website.

EXHIBIT III: EXTRACTS FROM PDI FINANCIAL STATEMENTS

PicDepot Inc.

Income Statement

For the Year Ended November 30, 2023

	2023 (unaudited)
Sales	$ 15,890,980
Operating expenses:	
Cost of sales – contributor royalties	$ 2,134,000
Discount on sales	975,000
Salaries and wages	4,593,849
General and administrative expenses	1,989,090
Stock options benefit expense	100,000
Income before taxes	$ 6,099,041
Income taxes	1,829,712
Net income	$ 4,269,329

EXHIBIT III (CONTINUED): EXTRACTS FROM PDI FINANCIAL STATEMENTS

PicDepot Inc.

Balance Sheet

For the Year Ended November 30, 2023

	2023 (unaudited)
	Assets
Current assets	
Cash	$ 7,250,000
Inventory – uploaded pictures/illustrations	15,000,000
Prepaid expenses	1,320,890
Due from related party	2,400
Property and equipment, net	1,500,700
Search software	1,160,000
Other assets	37,000
Total Assets	26,270,990
	Liabilities
Current liabilities	
Accounts payable	$ 5,098,289
Accrued liability	60,000
Total Liabilities	5,158,289
	Shareholders' Equity
Common shares	$ 1,000,000
Preferred shares	1,000,000
Retained earnings	19,112,701
Total Liabilities and Shareholders' Equity	26,270,990

PART 2

EXHIBIT IV: ADDITIONAL NOTES MADE BY LILLY BRUCE DURING THE PDI PRESENTATION

Recent Investments

On November 30, 2023, PDI purchased 100% of FabulousPic Inc. (FPI), a small private company that develops highly specialized software that allows users to modify images while keeping them looking extremely natural. FPI has great potential and a very talented young staff, however, it has not been well managed and was close to declaring bankruptcy before the takeover due to its inability to make debt payments. PDI paid $250,000 for FPI and also issued stock options (10,000 stock options in PDI vesting in 2028) to FPI's current owners as part of the purchase price. The exercise price is $25 per share. The fair value of net assets was assessed between $125,000 and $175,000. This investment was not yet recorded in PDI's financial statements.

In October 2023, Halley came across another investment opportunity. The owner of MyPhotoBox Inc. (MPBI), a private company, was retiring and since his family was not interested in taking over the business, he started looking for new investors. MPBI is an internet-based business that provides a range of personalized photo-based products and services. Revenue is generated mainly by producing and selling personalized, professionally bound photo albums and greeting cards. Halley immediately recognized this exciting opportunity, envisioning how the two companies would perfectly complement each other, but PDI only had the funds to purchase 15% of MPBI shares for $20 each. The deal closed on November 15 and was not yet recorded in PDI's financial statements. The owner told Halley that he is rushing to sell the company due to personal health concerns, and if he cannot find an interested investor, he will simply sell chunks of shares to smaller investors. As PDI was the first to invest, Halley was invited to find out more about the business by attending key management and board meetings.

On December 4, PDI purchased 5% (100,000 shares) in Image Ltd. (IL), a small public company. It was a bargain price of $2 per stock, as the stock was trading at $5 just a week before the purchase. At the time of purchase, allegations surfaced that IL "stole" another company's proprietary software, which was integral to IL's business. Presently, however, the stock has rebounded to $3.90, as the allegations appear to have been false. IL will be filing a lawsuit in the amount of $1,300,000 against those who made the allegations and IL is confident that this contingent gain will be recognized.

INTERMEDIATE FINANCIAL ACCOUNTING CASE 2

GreenSpace Inc.

GreenSpace Inc. is a cutting-edge company that focuses on making office spaces more suitable and productive for today's fast-paced environment. GreenSpace focuses primarily on furniture but goes beyond simple desks and chairs; it transforms workspaces by offering a range of innovative lounge chairs, standing desks, lie-down desks, etc. All its furniture ideas are sourced from talented freelance designers who sell their designs for a flat fee. Once GreenSpace purchases the right to a completed design, it can use the design as needed. At times, GreenSpace revises a particular design to suit a customer's specific needs.

The company was founded a couple of years ago by twin brothers—Jared and Jake Driver (who each own 50% of the shares). The brothers invested a small inheritance from their grandmother in the business. They also sourced some financing from a private investor and got a loan from a bank (the annual interest charged on the loan is 8%). Both the investor and the bank would like to see audited financial statements on an ongoing basis every year. The accounting has been done by a cousin of the brothers who had limited accounting skills and knowledge. Since the business grew substantially over the last couple of years, the cousin could not keep up with the business's demands and stepped down as GreenSpace's bookkeeper. After a difficult recruitment process, the brothers hired you, CPA.

Jared has booked all this year's journal entries. "While I passed all of my required accounting courses in university," he tells you. "I did not get very good marks and I know that my knowledge of accounting is poor. I expect I made a lot of errors booking some of the journal entries but I thought I'm better off trying than not. I would like you to focus on financial accounting issues over the next several weeks. I need a memo on my desk by tomorrow morning on any critical issues that you see with our accounting. I really didn't know how to book some of the transactions, so you'll have to establish appropriate accounting policies and book those transactions. We have to move fast as the auditors are coming in shortly to start the year-end audit. They told me they have a lot of questions about planning the audit and their audit procedures. We need to be prepared on our end by having proper accounting policies in place. Our fiscal year ends on April 30." Today is June 15, 2024.

On his way out, Jared says, "Almost forgot. I dealt with CPAs before—you're well trained to identify big-picture issues in all business areas. From a strategic perspective, are we on the right track? Do you think GreenSpace has made smart moves when it comes to growing the company and remaining profitable and successful? A couple of quick pointers wouldn't hurt. Why don't you include those in your memo as well?"

EXHIBIT I: NOTES FROM MEETING WITH JARED DRIVER

GreenSpace started out with two business lines: both ready-made and custom-made furniture formats. All furniture installation requires GreenSpace technicians' intimate understanding of how the furniture is assembled (e.g., a stand-up desk sold by GreenSpace can be quite complex to install). The main materials in the production of the furniture are steel, plastic, various fabrics, and glass.

New Distributor

Several big events occurred during the busy 2024 fiscal year. First, early in the year GreenSpace was approached by a young entrepreneur, Mitchell Hope. Mitchell said that he sees huge potential in his region's furniture market and asked the brothers if he could become a distributor of their ready-made furniture in the area. They immediately got along as all of them were entrepreneurs, and so the twins decided that a little help growing the business would not hurt. Mitchell incorporated a separate company called Hope Distributors Inc. (HDI). In May 2023, HDI ordered a shipment of ready-made furniture with a value of $2,000,000. As per the agreement, HDI pays Greenspace for the furniture once they sell each piece to a customer. HDI charges customers directly. Mitchell was trained on the installation of furniture so that he can hire and train his own installation crew in his area. While the payment is outstanding, no interest is charged by GreenSpace as the twins would like to see their new distributor succeed.

HDI does not do any advertising on its own and relies on the advertising done by GreenSpace. For example, a Nova Scotia–based customer might contact GreenSpace after discovering some furniture of interest on the website, and she will be directed to arrange the furniture's shipment and installation through HDI. Jared mentioned that several referrals have been made by Hope Distributors Inc. Prices are not quoted on the GreenSpace website, as each combination of furniture will be sold at a different price point. If there are problems with the furniture, the purchaser would have to address any issues directly with GreenSpace, not HDI, which provides a 3-year warranty on all of its products. No journal entries have been booked pertaining to HDI.

New Product – Software

While Jake was at university studying IT and psychology, he developed proprietary software that accurately tracks productivity in the workplace. While many people tried developing similar software, none had achieved the same level of accuracy and thoroughness. This year, Jake sold the software to GreenSpace. GreenSpace will pay Jake $200,000 for the software over 30 months.

Shortly after purchasing Jake's software, GreenSpace began to commercialize and monetize it. The software allows companies to measure their productivity before and after any major organizational changes take place. For example, if a company's management changes its office layout, furniture, and other attributes of the physical workspace, the software is able to measure employee's productivity before the change and then again six months after. The first outside company to use the software found the tool to be invaluable and word quickly spread among the business community. Not only did the furniture business significantly increase (as the reorganizing of the office space was shown to have made a significant positive impact on employees' productivity), but now other companies wanted to purchase the software as well.

By the end of the year, several clients had signed a contract to license the software. A number of them were solely interested in the license and not in the furniture itself. Customers can subscribe to purchase the licensing rights for two years. At the end of the term, they can either choose to discontinue using the asset or renew it for another two years. Customers can renew for as many periods as they like but they must commit for no less than two years each renewal. Support and maintenance are available to all license subscribers for the license term. The subscription period for the license and the maintenance period commence once the contract is signed with the customer, regardless of whether the customer starts using the license right away. Within each term period (i.e., within two years), GreenSpace is committed, as per the contract, to provide at least one upgrade to the software subsequent to its initial release. Management expects that about 10% of customers will not renew at all and most customers will renew between two and five times. Payments for the software license are made by customers when the licensing contract is signed. No revenue has been recorded in relation to the license, as Jared was not sure how to apply the new accounting rules here.

Jake is really excited about this new development. Since most clients purchasing the software are medium to large corporations, he believes that this will allow GreenSpace to quickly penetrate the market. However, he still wants to do whatever he can to get the software out into the market as soon as possible. Getting the word out quickly is important, as they anticipate that new companies will soon start copying the software. To that end, GreenSpace hired 10 salespeople whose job was to solely promote the software. Every time a customer is signed up for two years, the salesperson receives a 10% commission. When the commission is paid, the journal entry made is Dr. Commission Expense, Cr. Cash. No commission is received by the salesperson if the client renews the license subscription.

Business Challenges

Jared and Jake noticed that no matter how unique their ideas for better working spaces are, eventually the market catches up and offers similar products. Therefore, every year, GreenSpace introduces several new furniture items. However, they are not able to warehouse all furniture models, so some are slowly phased out. While it is GreenSpace's policy to never hold furniture sales, the slow phase-out strategy allows them to successfully dispose of old models. As the new furniture is being produced, GreenSpace stops production of the older pieces and retires the design. To preserve the GreenSpace brand, the design is never to be used again and is not resold.

Given that the software business has been doing quite well, the brothers sat down and took a hard look at all current business lines in the furniture industry. They decided that, with its lower margins, custom-made furniture was too specialized a business and that ready-made furniture is the way to go. While most of the manufacturing equipment used to produce the custom-made furniture is also used to produce ready-made furniture, there is some specialized equipment needed for the custom-made pieces. The brothers contacted a dealer who specializes in buying and selling specialized equipment. The seller said that he is fine with removing and storing GreenSpace's unused equipment while he looks for a potential buyer. He will be asking $150,000 for the equipment on behalf of GreenSpace and he charges a 2.5% commission. If the equipment is not sold within six months, it will be returned to GreenSpace, as the dealer is not interested in keeping it on the premises for longer due to low interest from potential customers. At that point, GreenSpace will have to find another dealer. GreenSpace retains the legal title to the equipment while it is on the dealer's premises. When the equipment was shipped to the dealer, Jared booked the following journal entry: Dr. AR; Cr. Revenue $150,000. It has been five months since the equipment was removed from GreenSpace, and the dealer said that because some of the equipment is quite old, he has not seen much interest. Most companies that look for this type of equipment want to buy the latest technology. If the equipment was sold for scrap only (which is not what this dealer specializes in), it would be sold for $15,000.

To equip their 10 new salespeople with the best possible resources, GreenSpace leased a couple of vehicles for five years for $450/month per vehicle and some laptops for $250/month per laptop. All vehicles and laptops are secondhand. Six of the 10 salespeople expressed interest in using their own laptops and cars instead of having GreenSpace lease these from a third-party. Jared wants to make sure that the employees are happy and believes that this will be an even more convenient option as long as the employees don't mind it being a taxable benefit to them. Therefore, instead of paying the rental fees directly to the dealers for the leased items, the amounts are just added to the employee payroll every month and paid out to them. The journal entry for all payments to dealers and employees is made at the time of payment, Dr. Operating Expense, Cr. Cash. No other journal entries have been made.

GreenSpace also rented out its first retail location in the suburbs. Jared and Jake felt the retail space was necessary since they needed a physical space to display their innovative furniture and space arrangements. Jared said that he spent some time looking for a proper location and used a real estate agent who was eventually paid $5,000 for his services. The rent is $4,000 per month, plus 3% of sales made out of the store. Jared does not expect any sales being made directly at the store, but it would be a place where contracts would be signed. Jared says that, since the contract is vague on whether sales include "sale contracts signed" or just "direct sales," he is not planning to pay the 3%. When discussing this he says to you, "They cannot check this stuff in any case. . . . It's not like auditors dig that deeply." GreenSpace's retail space was formerly a restaurant, so they had to spend $15,000 reconfiguring the space. The lessor promised to pay one third of that cost but has not yet done so. GreenSpace has the right to terminate the five-year rental agreement at any point by paying a penalty of $8,000. Unfortunately, Jared says that the store has experienced very low traffic, so they are planning to increase advertising. The lessor required a deposit payment of $12,000 to cover the first three months of payment. Regular payments will commence at the beginning of the fourth month. All of the payments are expensed as incurred.

Jared tells you that the former bookkeeper used to book the following journal entry when a furniture design is purchased from independent designers: Dr. Design Rights, Cr. Cash. Jared booked the same journal entry when another two designs were purchased this year. On average, GreenSpace pays $15,000 per design and the company has purchased 30 designs over its history.

EXHIBIT II: EXCERPT FROM GREENSPACE FINANCIAL STATEMENTS

Cash	$	389,560
Accounts receivable	$	2,644,187
Inventory	$	5,465,879
Design rights	$	450,000
Notes receivable - Hope Distributors Inc.	$	2,000,000
Equipment - custom-made furniture (net of amortization)	$	160,000
Equipment - ready-made furniture (net of amortization)	$	300,000
Total Assets		**11,409,626**

INTERMEDIATE FINANCIAL ACCOUNTING CASE 3

"Cooper"/Michizini Media Inc.

Adrian Michizini founded Michizini Media Inc. (MMI) 20 years ago when he created a character named "Cooper," a friendly bear whose life is tracked in a cartoon series from birth to late adolescence. The series is both witty and educational and is popular with parents and kids alike. According to a recent article in a major newspaper that examined the trends of child-oriented media, "Cooper is a classic of 'old television,' when kids would gather around the TV to laugh and learn. No violence, no excessive action, no out-of-this-world unrealistic story lines. This is the kind of TV that our kids need more of today."

MMI currently has three lines of business:

- Licensing the Cooper cartoon to TV broadcasters (all contracts are negotiated individually)
- Manufacturing Cooper plush toys (sold to retailers at an average price of $7)
- Manufacturing a Cooper clothing line (clothing items are sold to retailers at an average price of $15)

At the beginning of the current fiscal year, Adrian expanded the business with the goal of going public soon. An investment firm invested $30 million in the company on September 2, 2022. The firm liked Adrian's growth plan as well as the security associated with Cooper's strong brand recognition. MMI no longer produces any new Cooper cartoons, as it was a natural stopping point when the character reached adulthood. Realizing how heavily MMI depends on Cooper's success, Adrian is developing two new characters in an attempt to build a similar following. Adrian also has a vision of building a small indoor Cooper theme park.

Today is May 9, 2023. You, CPA, have been hired as MMI's CFO. The old CFO retired 10 months ago after feeling overwhelmed by the new developments. Adrian made it clear that it is your responsibility to set up accounting policies for the events that took place this fiscal year and to give the financial statements a general clean up. Adrian asked you to outline all new accounting policies in a memo.

"We will be under a fair amount of scrutiny once we decide to go public," he says. "I know that we can't foresee everything, but I want you to take a hard look at our operations and tell me if there is anything that needs to be addressed. Don't forget, your first priority is to assess the accounting issues."

Since MMI's financial year ended on April 30, you have to get to work right away. You have asked to meet with your colleagues from the executive team so that you can be quickly brought up to speed. Adrian did not attend the meeting, as you had already been introduced while touring the office on the first day of work at MMI. Your assistant, Nancy, took notes during the meeting. Accounting manager Willow Kirk, who will be reporting to you, also joined the meeting.

EXHIBIT I: NOTES TAKEN BY NANCY DURING THE MEETING WITH THE EXECUTIVE TEAM

Present: Willow Kirk (Accounting Manager), Nancy Lano (Executive Assistant), Brian Gladwell (Chief Strategy Officer), Lucas D'Angelo (Creative Director), and Harley McDonald (Human Resources Manager)

Brian: "As you know, Cooper is our pride and joy. His character had an excellent 20-year run. Our Cooper-related sales, such as licensing the cartoon to broadcasters and our merchandising revenue, have grown steadily during this time. However, this is the first year that sales are flat. We don't know whether it's a temporary slowdown, as trends are always unpredictable. We're considering doing a study of market trends and assessing Cooper's popularity, but we already know that overall the industry is still growing. We've talked to our retailers who purchase Cooper merchandise for resale, and they've indicated that some of the merchandise was discounted to get it moving out of their stores. We continue to produce merchandise at our normal production levels for now."

Lucas: "In the meantime, this has been an exciting year for us. We began the creative process related to two new shows: 'Tommy and Polly' and 'Pat-the-Rat.' Each show has its own approach. For Tommy and Polly, we hired a team of animators and scriptwriters who came up with several characters and story lines. After extensive research with our target audience, children aged 7 to 12, we decided to go with the Tommy and Polly idea. The cartoon is about the relationship between a brother and sister and their adventures growing up."

"I have to say, this is a really tough business. Not only do we need to get our story line right, but the presentation of the characters is very critical as well. We chose from five versions of Tommy and Polly created by our cartoonists. We hired voice actors, including some amazing Hollywood stars, to voice the characters of Tommy and Polly. The pilot episode aired two months ago and it was approved to air on a major TV channel next fall. I think the entire project cost us less than $500,000 but I'm not certain: we don't follow strict budgets here and tracking costs is sometimes difficult, as our staff are busy with several things at once."

Willow moves a piece of paper towards you and says, "Here's a summary of the costs that we've incurred so far" (see Exhibit II).

Brian: "We intend to provide short-term renewable licenses to broadcast the Tommy and Polly cartoon, as opposed to selling the rights to it. We hope to break even in the second year and become profitable via licensing revenue starting in the third. Since we also need to show our investors some immediate returns, we're going to sell the Pat-the-Rat series once it's ready. We believe that several TV broadcasters might be interested but we haven't pitched the show yet. We're not very far along with the Pat-the-Rat project but we acquired the rights to the character from an independent cartoonist. The pilot's script was developed internally and was approved by Adrian. We will start producing the pilot shortly."

"And let's not forget about our new line of business: educational 'cue cards' aimed at young kids. The cards come in a book-like format that can be taken apart and used before being reassembled back into a book. It's an interactive tool intended to teach the ABCs and numbers up to 100. The manuscripts, artwork, and layout were created and edited a year ago. We haven't done much with it this year given everything else that is going on. However, we sent out the cards to a large sample of kindergarten teachers for feedback."

Willow: "The sample test run of the cue cards cost us $560,000!"

Brian: "Yes, but we received a ton of positive feedback and several schools expressed interest in the cards. We were worried that if the feedback was negative we would need to delay production and make some changes. I'm glad that was not the case."

Willow: "I'm very happy about this as well. . . this has been a cash drain for a while!"

Brian: "Well, let's not forget that we're hoping to make the cue cards part of the educational curriculum in at least two provinces. We're very close to signing with the respective education boards. Once that's accomplished, we're considering releasing an online version. With all the subsequent editions and reiterations, I'm hoping to squeeze at least 20 years out of this 'investment,' just like we did with Cooper!"

Lucas: "Cooper's longevity is really a miracle! Most cartoon characters don't survive so long, aside from a few exceptions. You never know what's around the corner. Trends are so fleeting."

Willow: "As Adrian already probably mentioned to you, we borrowed $30 million for the expansion. About $10 million was specifically allocated to the Tommy and Polly project, as the lenders really liked these two characters. Another $12 million was budgeted for the indoor Cooper theme park and the rest is meant to support our overall growth. An annual interest rate of 6% is paid on the loan's anniversary date (i.e., September 2 of each year)." [*Brian notices the puzzled expression on your face.*] "Oh! We completely forgot to tell you about the indoor Cooper centre! This is very exciting. Since bad weather is prevalent in Canada, we opted for an indoor centre instead of an outdoor park. The original plan was to get the centre running in January, but luck was not on our side during construction. First, it took us a while to find the right location. Construction didn't commence until November 1, 2022, a month behind schedule. Second, the building contractors took almost all of December off due to unusually heavy snowfalls and the holidays. The centre opened on March 1, but a small food court was still under construction. Thankfully, construction was completed by April 30 (you know how important it is to have a food court where kids can get their special treats!) and we're now fully operational. The only problem is that we're a bit short on staff, so many people have to work overtime."

Harley: "Oh, that's good to know. I'll make sure we go on a hiring spree right away. If we start now, we can get the new staff up and running in eight weeks. That doesn't include training though. It would be 10 weeks, including training."

The meeting is adjourned for 10 minutes to obtain refreshments. During the break you ask Willow about some of the accounts on the balance sheet (see Exhibit II). She gives you a quick summary:

- The only items currently in inventory are the Cooper merchandise.
- All Tommy and Polly and Pat-the-Rat related costs are included as part of "production costs."
- The majority of cue card book-related expenses occurred last fiscal year. Before the previous CFO retired, he carefully analyzed all costs and capitalized only the applicable development costs. This fiscal year, the only relevant expenses relate to the sample copies sent out to educators, which have been capitalized. Commercial production of the product began last month.
- All interest costs incurred on the $30 million loan were included in the "other assets" line item.
- It costs about $3 to produce a plush toy and $5 to produce a clothing item.

The meeting resumes:

Brian: "Since we are constantly looking for ways to further grow the Cooper brand, this year we welcomed any partnership opportunities that came our way. We were asked by a large toy store, Hapleys, to participate in the launch week of one of its new stores. They wanted us to deliver a Cooper–Hapleys co-branded mascot. As part of this contract, we were responsible for several things. First, we had to manufacture the co-branded mascot. Since I've had some poor experiences with these types of arrangements (e.g., a client cancelling at the last minute), I asked Hapleys to include a clause in the contract that ensures they will be consulted on the mascot's design, etc., and Hapleys can terminate the contract if they are unsatisfied with our performance at any point in time. In the event of a terminated contract, Hapleys will be responsible for paying for the work completed up to that point. Second, we were responsible for hiring someone to wear a mascot costume and ensuring that they appeared at the store for a two-week period. The mascot was to give away 5,000 Cooper-Hapleys co-branded mini-Cooper plush toys and 1,000 T-shirts, which were delivered as part of the contract. The launch began April 21 and ended May 5. MMI provided the mascot, plush toys, and T-shirts. For all of this, Hapleys paid a flat fee of $65,000 on May 5. The event was a huge success and we expect that this partnership will only grow and result in more similar events. Any remaining toys and T-shirts were kept by Hapleys. It's only fair, since they paid for them!"

Willow: "By the way, we haven't recognized this transaction on the financial statements. Also, you should know that we have an excellent relationship with Hapleys. They are the only retailer that hasn't reduced their purchasing volumes with us in the last few months."

EXHIBIT II: SUMMARY OF COSTS INCURRED FOR THE TOMMY AND POLLY PROJECT

Market research (audience demographic)	$	15,000
Scriptwriter salaries (including work completed for the pilot)	$	80,000
Cartoonists salaries (including work completed for the pilot)	$	100,000
Voice-over casting	$	20,000
Voice-over (including work completed for the pilot)	$	50,000
Adrian's salary	$	300,000
Production of pilot episode (including administrative expenses)	$	50,000
Music composition	$	15,000
Register broadcast rights	$	2,000
	$	632,000

EXHIBIT III: DISCUSSION WITH ADRIAN MICHIZINI

As you leave the meeting, you run into Adrian, who says, "Hope the meeting with your new colleagues went well!"

He invites you into this office and says,

> Listen, I need your help with some advice for an old friend. It won't take long, I just need some quick pointers. My friend, Sandy, recently bought a lamb farm. She and her husband own it but she wants to get some bank financing to grow the business. She thinks her current accountant, who follows accounting standards suitable for public enterprises, isn't accounting correctly for a number of things, and she wants me to ask you about these accounting issues.
>
> To start, Sandy bought 50 baby lambs. She bought an old farm with a barn, but she still had to purchase hay for the lambs' bedding. She feeds them rations of grains and minerals designed for the animals' optimal health. Clean water is also a necessity, so Sandy purchased automatic waterers, an expensive system that is supposed to last 10 years or so.
>
> When the lambs mature into adults, Sandy plans to use about half for wool production and half for dairy production. Eventually, she might use some sheep for meat production as well but for now she wants to stick to just wool and dairy production. There's an active year-round market for lamb and sheep alike. Sandy tells me that a lamb's price is determined by its weight. However, some farmers are willing to accept a lower selling price if the buyers come directly to their farm. I mentioned to her that this would also mean that she can charge a premium for "farm-fresh" lambs.
>
> One sheep produces anywhere from 2 to 30 pounds of wool annually. In 2023, the average price paid for wool sold in Canada was $1.10 per pound.
>
> Sandy's current accountant capitalized the lambs purchased at their cost and has been expensing all of the costs I just referred to. Sandy wonders whether this is correct.
>
> By the way, did you know that sheep were apparently domesticated 10,000 years ago? That's how old sheep farming is! Anyways, please prepare a memo for me on any relevant accounting issues I can pass on to Sandy.

EXHIBIT IV: EXTRACTS FROM MMI'S FINANCIAL STATEMENTS

	As of April 31, 2023, in thousands	As of December 31, 2022, in thousands
ASSETS		
Current		
Cash	$ 6,404	$ 5,132
Accounts and other receivables	12,029	10,238
Inventories	9,857	2,361
Production costs	2,500	1,592
Deferred income taxes	1,151	746
Other assets	1,443	1,191
Total Current Assets	33,384	21,260
Attractions, building, and equipment	64,118	64,118
Other tangible assets	9,042	9,042
Land	1,875	1,857
Intangible assets	10,758	11,151
Total Assets	119,177	107,428
LIABILITIES AND EQUITY		
Current		
Accounts payable and other accrued liabilities	$ 11,766	$ 11,393
Current portion of borrowings	6,843	1,890
Total Current Liabilities	18,609	13,283
Borrowings	48,236	1,379
Deferred income taxes	6,076.5	6,147
Other long-term liabilities	203	205
Commitments and contingencies		
Total Liabilities	73,124.5	21,014
Common shares	15,000	15,000
Retained Earnings	31,051	71,412
Total Equity	$ 46,051	86,412
Total Liabilities and Equity	119,175.5	107,426

INTERMEDIATE FINANCIAL ACCOUNTING CASE 4

Möbel Inc.

Derek Wolf, a young entrepreneur who grew up watching his father build a business from the ground up, has just stepped into his new role as the CEO of Möbel Inc. Möbel, started by Derek's father Niklas Wolf, sells furniture out of seven locations across the country. When Niklas immigrated to Canada in 1965, the market for European furniture was not well-developed and he immediately saw a niche.

Until recently, Niklas, who is now 87 years old, has been quite active in the business but his quickly deteriorating health required him to step down as CEO.

Today is July 31, 2023, and Derek invited you, CPA and consultant, to help with multiple issues. "I know so little about accounting," admits Derek. "I generally don't like numbers that much. I have a degree in Strategy and Entrepreneurship from the University of Cambridge. While I finished my degree with distinction, accounting has never been my friend, so I need your help with accounting and numbers in general. Specifically, I need you to help me establish accounting policies to be used in the preparation of our financial statements for the first six months of this fiscal year (i.e., from January 1 to June 30). Dad stepped down on June 30. Also, please explain to me the implications of going ahead with my new vision and strategy, which is outlined in this presentation (see Exhibit II). How will these economic activities be accounted for in the statements if we implement the new strategy?"

You set up a meeting with Derek to find out what has been happening for the past half a year (see Exhibit I) and to discuss Derek's vision. The company's year-end is December 31. There are plans to take Möbel public as soon as the company is ready.

EXHIBIT I: EXTRACTS FROM MEETING MINUTES WITH DEREK WOLF

Competitive Environment

Currently, Möbel operates seven stores across the country, selling European-style household furniture. Derek believes that Möbel enjoys approximately 5% of the furniture market share. Lately, big-box stores have been consolidating. However, there are still many smaller chains and individual stores in the market. The pricing competition is more intense than the competition in quality. Big sales in the furniture industry usually begin right before the beginning of the school year (i.e., back-to-school sales season) and continue into the fall.

All of the land and buildings where Möbel stores operate are company owned. Niklas has always been proud of the real estate portfolio that he built into the company. However, he has always emphasized that the company's true asset is its employees. The sales staff were trained not to "push sales" but to act as consultants and trusty advisors, and work to build long-term relationships with clients. Sales staff have always worked on commission.

Given the competitive furniture market, Niklas decided at the beginning of this year to offer warranties, marketed as the "Worry-Free Family Warranty" plan. The first year of the warranty is usually covered by the manufacturer but the subsequent four years are now covered by Möbel. If the furniture breaks, customers who purchased the warranty can have it repaired or replaced, if it cannot be fixed. The Worry-Free Family Warranty costs $200 per piece of furniture. If a family purchases a living room set, it averages out at five individual furniture pieces. The salesperson who sells the warranty will receive a 30% commission from the warranty plan price. A commission on the sale of a $1,000 warranty on a five-piece set would equal $300. This is a significant commission given that normally sales staff receive just 4% from furniture sales.

Another initiative, implemented in April 2023 and intended to distinguish Möbel from the competition, was to provide a price guarantee. Even though Möbel makes every attempt to offer unique furniture for the best price, the same pieces do pop up from time to time at various other retailers. Niklas was expecting this trend to continue and, as a fearless competitor, he decided to provide customers with a price-matching guarantee. If claimed within 90 days of purchase, Möbel customers can receive a refund for the difference between the price they paid for a piece of furniture and a competitor's current price, or if the piece goes on sale after the initial purchase. So far, only a handful of customers across Canada have taken advantage of this offer.

New Vision

Derek agrees with Niklas that the retail environment is becoming more competitive and that new initiatives are essential. However, he disagrees about the kind of changes that need to be implemented. Sometime ago, Derek prepared a presentation to make his case to Niklas. His dad was not persuaded by his approach, and until he assumed the role of CEO, Derek was unable to implement his changes. Derek's main idea is to diversify revenues and grow the brand name.

Derek gave you the presentation slides, as well as the accompanying notes. (Derek made a couple of updates to the slides since he presented it to his dad.) Now that he is at liberty to do as he wishes, he is planning to implement the proposed changes. Derek updated the slides before giving them to you. He says, "You'll see I also proposed some key performance indicators that will allow us to measure Möbel World's success! Do you think these are good measures? I'd be glad to hear your thoughts on these and any other recommendations for other indicators we could employ."

EXHIBIT II: EXTRACTS FROM DEREK WOLF'S PRESENTATION

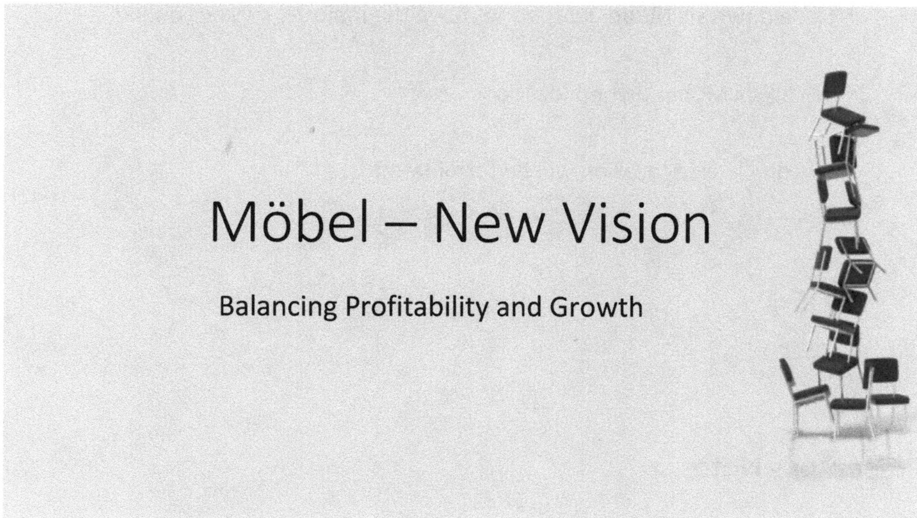

Presenter's Notes

Welcome to the future of Möbel.

Online sales

- Close down six Möbel stores and move the majority of sales online
- Sell all six Möbel-owned locations
- The one leased location will be terminated

Presenter's Notes

Möbel will close down six of seven stores. One of these six locations is a leased location, and Möbel will have to continue paying lease payments for the next 10 months. We cannot sublease the location for such a short duration. The monthly lease payment is $22,000.

As per the balance sheet, the average cost of each real estate property currently held by Möbel is $250,000. Möbel will be able to sell each property for $700,000. This means that we will have ($700,000 - $250,000) × 6 = $3,000,000 available in financing for Möbel's future growth.

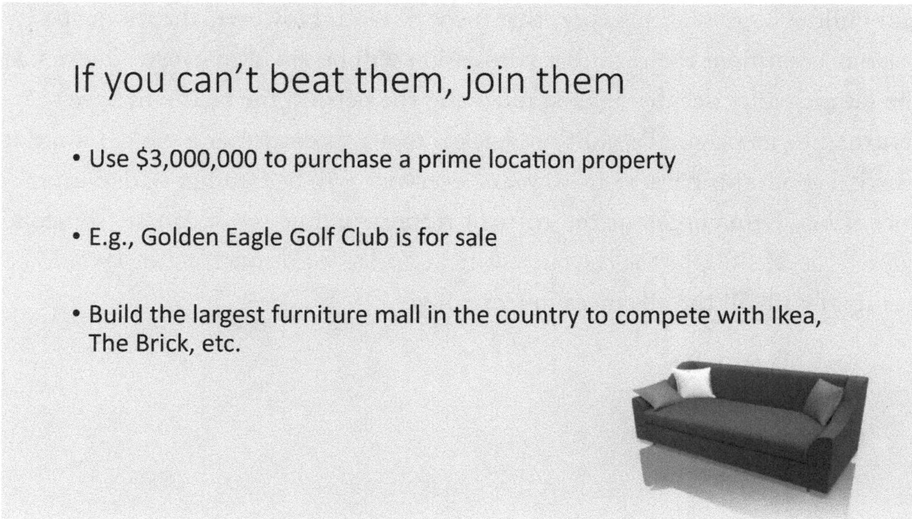

Presenter's Notes

Even though we are moving the majority of our sales online, I believe we should still have a brick-and-mortar location to not only strengthen our brand name, but to make it more well-known. Since giants like Ikea and The Brick are crowding out the smaller chains, I believe we must combine our forces. I am proposing that Möbel build a large furniture mall in the area and rent out its space to other small to mid-size furniture chains. Customers will no longer need to visit Ikea when they can instead visit Möbel World. By the way, the name "Möbel World" is not accidental. It will boost our name recognition! Of course, Möbel will also have a store in the mall.

I expect our financing from the sale of our stores will be sufficient to cover the expenses for the mall's construction. If we run short, we can start selling mall spaces before it is complete, instead of renting them out later. It is uncertain at this point and will depend on market conditions. I am definitely set on not borrowing money from the bank. Before we decide whether the units will be sold or rented, I would like to get the board's opinion. I am firmly leaning towards the rent model, which will ensure a continuous stream of revenue for us.

I want the location to be central. Since we require a very large piece of land and the city is overbuilt as it is, I had to think creatively. The Golden Eagle Golf Club is currently for sale. This is a prime real estate location and right in the middle of the city, making it accessible to all GTA customers. I held preliminary discussions with the municipality and they will allow us to rezone and build a large mall plaza on that piece of land. However, the municipality has one condition: the rezoning permission will be assessed every 30 years. If the municipality decides against renewing the permit, the land will have to be returned to its original condition, back into a golf course or a park. I am not worried about this because in 30 years, everyone will be familiar with our presence. Plus, I am confident the costs of reconstructing a golf course (someone quoted me $1,000,000 as the current ticket price for reconstruction) would be minimal with all the advances in technology.

So long brick-and-mortar stores!

- Timeline:
  - August 2023 – announce plan to close six out of seven brick-and-mortar stores to staff
  - September 2023 – close four out of seven stores
  - October 2023 – contact a prestigious real estate agency and put the remaining stores up for sale (large commercial properties can take up to four months to sell)
  - January 2024 – close remaining two out of seven stores
  - February 2024 – complete sale of the real estate properties

Presenter's Notes

The above illustrates the action plan's timeline. Note that all in-store equipment (e.g., shelving units, cash registers) will be sold since we will not need them. We're going to be selling furniture online! I expect the transition to be seamless.

Hello Möbel World!

- Timeline (UPDATED):
  - February 2024 – construction commences
  - January 2025 – sales office opens, sales people hired, and Möbel World advertises to potential vendors to reserve their space
  - December 2025 – one-month break for construction crew – construction is halted
  - November 2026 – allow 50% of tenants access premises to customize their stores, make cosmetic improvements to premises as appropriate
  - January 2027 – allow remaining tenants access to premises
  - February 2027 – open doors to customers on weekends ONLY (while continuing to complete minor work on building during the week)
  - March 2027 – open doors to customers seven days a week

Presenter's Notes

The timeline above gives a better idea of our projected milestones. I firmly believe that an integral part of our vision should be continuing to stay invested in real estate property and allow tenants to rent our premises.

We expect 25 tenants will occupy the Möbel World mall. The tenants will start their payments once they get access to the premises as per the schedule presented here. We will establish an appropriate price based on the competition's rates. An average lease will be for a three year duration. To incentivize tenants to take a chance on this great opportunity, we will be providing $100,000 in unrestricted cash, which is intended to enable them to carry out cosmetic changes to their stores. We will also be providing maintenance and security services. Our security office and property management office (both quite small) will be located directly in the mall, so that if our vendors have any questions, they can be answered right away.

We will hire the best salespeople in town and give them a generous budget, so that they don't just stay in the office but hit the road to recruit the best vendors available. We want Möbel World to be known for its quality vendors. Building up the Möbel World name will be key—we want to be known as the place people can trust for fairly priced and high-quality furniture.

Purchase of Design-on-Your-Terms

- Design-on-Your-Terms is a software that allows customers to enter the dimensions of their living space into the software and virtually try out various pieces of furniture
- Purchased the Design-on-Your-Terms software in January 2023 for $1,200,000
- UPDATE: No comparable software on the market until July 2023; a start-up company just released their software, called CreativeDesign 1.0, which has similar functionalities to Design-on-Your-Terms software; the company has approached Möbel and other furniture stores to license their software

Presenter's Notes

As part of our new strategy to diversify revenues, we would like to license the Design-on-Your-Terms software. The idea is that every vendor in Möbel World will have an in-store computer with software that they will license from us. The software will incorporate the inventory offered by the various vendors who signed up for its use. The idea is simple: since it is common for a customer to purchase a bookshelf from one store and a sofa from another, we want to make it convenient for customers to put their own décor together virtually to see how it looks together. Customers are more likely to buy more when they feel excited about the end result and the fulfillment of their vision. Therefore, while it will not be mandatory for retailers to license our software, I believe once a few sign on, the rest will follow suit as otherwise they will simply be losing out.

The retailers would pay a one-time fee of $50,000 for the 10-year license, which can afterwards be renewed in five-year increments. This fee includes regular maintenance to the software to resolve any "bugs," but does not include upgrades (i.e., any new software versions). The latter would be purchased for $50 per month. We will commit to releasing a maintenance update for at least each quarter. (We will ensure that this relatively low cost is heavily marketed to our retailers as it is my understanding that software companies normally charge at least $400 per year for such maintenance.) We will hire two full-time, high-performing IT people out of a top university to develop the software upgrades. Their salaries would not exceed $70,000 each for the initial couple of years. Once purchased, the software can be used at any of the retailers' store locations (i.e., not limited to Möbel World). However, only this software will be allowed for use at Möbel World.

Presenter's Notes

We will make it as easy as possible for vendors to rent a space. As I mentioned, they are truly our customers now and we want to make sure that the service they receive from us is efficient and exceptional.

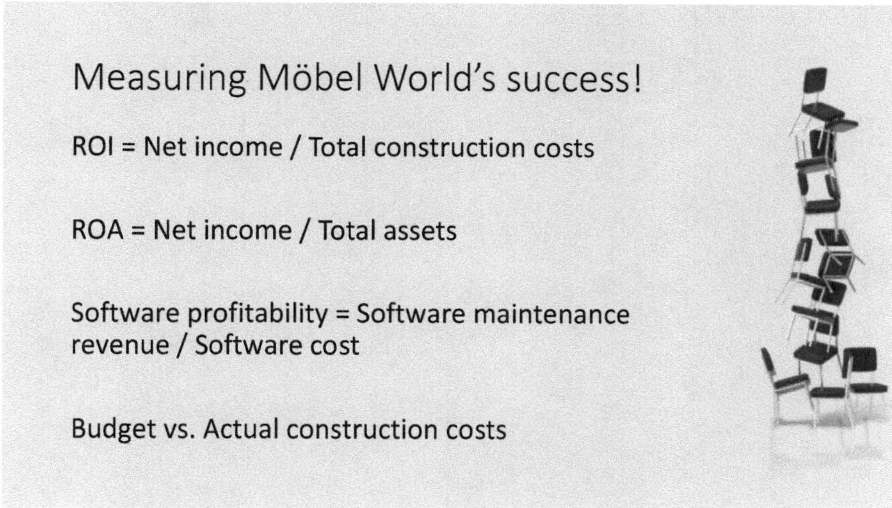

Presenter's Notes

These are the key financial performance indicators that we are planning to use to measure Möbel World's success. Figures such as net income and total assets will be taken directly off the financial statements for simplicity. The software cost is the net book value that the software is reported at.

PART FOUR

Audit Cases

AUDIT CASE 1

WorldConnect Inc.

WorldConnect Inc. (WCI) is a large express carrier that specializes in delivering packages across the world. The company was founded by Mr. and Mrs. Andrew in 1988 when they bought a small airplane to ship expensive items from England to Canada. The company is owned by the Andrew family, as well as a few small passive investors. WCI currently offers ground and air freight services in over 120 countries.

It is now November 9, 2023, and WCI's year-end is September 30. You, CPA, are an audit manager at Teller & Associates and have recently met with the engagement partner, Lisa, who explained the following: "CPA, WCI has been a long-time client of the firm and due to a recent application for a bank loan, they are going to require an audit of their financial statements. WCI complies with accounting standards suitable for private enterprises. Please prepare the preliminary audit planning memo as well as identify any internal control weaknesses."

After the meeting, you did some research on the company's activities and your notes are presented below:

CPA'S RESEARCH NOTES

Given strong competition in the industry, WCI has built prominent brand recognition for its 100% delivery guarantee of expensive items such as antiques, heirlooms, and jewelry. If an item is lost or stolen en route, WCI guarantees the client will be reimbursed. While WCI has always heavily focused on preventing theft, some packages continue to arrive empty to their destinations in 2023. To receive the reimbursement (which is equivalent to the fair value of a lost or stolen item), the client has to file a complaint and WCI usually resolves it within 3 months. Currently, WCI faces a backlog of complaints as the reimbursement clerk is on maternity leave and most of the outstanding cases are expected to take up to one year to resolve. Traditionally, WCI spends at least $250,000 annually on recompensation. However, management anticipates that the expense will double, as this fiscal year was an exceptional year for theft due to the economic downturn.

To mitigate the risk of packages arriving empty, WCI implemented a system where, prior to sending out a package for shipment, the contents of the package are cross-checked with the sales order and documented in the system. Due to the flexibility of staff duties, there is no designated staff member responsible for this, as it is a shared responsibility across the company. When performing the walk through, I noticed that approximately one out of three orders have been checked prior to shipment.

WCI management has instructed its Research and Development (R&D) department to come up with a solution to the theft problem. The R&D team has spent $250,000 researching new ideas, which included trips to Europe to "follow the packages' journey." The team also spent $450,000 developing one of the ideas, a monitoring device that can sense whether the package is being opened and will send a distress signal to the control room at the WCI's headquarters. The R&D team expects to spend no more than $50,000 to finish up this project, since the device's first testing was successful.

While WCI leases most of its airplanes, it currently owns five smaller planes, including a corporate jet. Prior to the pandemic, each plane (except for the corporate jet) made 240 trips per year, generating $40,000 in annual revenues. Due to the economic/COVID-19 crisis beginning in 2020, management decided at the beginning of 2023 to temporarily ground five company-owned planes and continue using the leased planes instead. Their airplanes were originally purchased in 2019 for $350,000 each (WCI received a discount on the purchase) and were amortized on a straight-line basis over 10 years. The WCI executive chose not to sell the planes on the open market, as they believe the prices to be currently quite low: each plane could only be sold for approximately $330,000 to $370,000, depending on its age and condition.

WCI's main sorting facility in Canada underwent a major overhaul in 2023. Since WCI decided not to replace the sorting equipment that was purchased in 2018, major work was needed, including updating the sorting software and replacing some of the conveyors, weight scales, and code recognition readers. WCI incurred $500,000 for the overhaul, which also included an inspection of the entire system for free.

To ensure all products are secure during the shipment process, WCI has implemented a state-of-the-art security system in their storage facility that can only be accessed by authorized personnel. To enter the facility, an employee must use an access card. During a tour of the facility, management explained how products held there are properly tracked. A tagging system is used to track products, with those that are ready to be processed for shipping tagged with a blue slip. All products that have been returned by customers and that are to be sent back to the original manufacturers are tagged with a yellow slip.

In response to increased competition in the freight industry, WCI wanted to diversify its portfolio. In the beginning of this fiscal year the economy started gaining momentum again and WCI decided to purchase 15% of GlobalHome Inc. Since WCI had some idle cash at the time, management decided to buy the stock at a low price hoping to sell it at a higher price over the next year. GlobalHome owns and operates luxury hotels in remote parts of the world and has a very strong track record. In fact, the company has been extremely profitable despite the economic downturn and its share price has been rising. WCI management also wanted their pilots to have a "home" hotel in every part of the world. Currently, WCI pilots do not receive any discounts if they stay at one of the GlobalHome hotels, but the two companies are now in negotiations. This investment has not yet been recorded on the financial statements and WCI is relying on the auditors to book this transaction.

Beginning in 2022, WCI implemented a new checkout system for those customers who wish to arrange for a package pickup. This new process was well-received by customers, as the system allows customers to keep all their credit card information and shipping address on file. Management is thrilled with the checkout process, as it can be accessed by anyone around the world quickly using the internet. Even if an individual has never ordered from WCI before, they are still able to create a profile, input their information, and request a package pickup within the same day.

Prior to year-end, one of WCI's largest customers placed an order for delivery that was to be completed in October 2023. Due to the delivery's unusually large amount of products, WCI requested a 25% deposit upon the contract being signed. At year-end, the entire amount of the deposit has been recognized as revenue.

WorldConnect Inc.
Unconsolidated Income Statement
For the Year Ended September 30, 2023

	(unaudited)
Revenue	
Revenue	$ 10,000,000
Cost of goods sold	5,600,000
Gross margin	4,400,000
Expenses	
General and administrative expense	$ 450,000
Research and development expense	750,000
Compensation for lost/stolen items expense	500,000
Employee and executive salaries expense	650,000
Airplane expense	800,000
Airplane impairment expense	1,400,000
Repair and maintenance expense	500,000
Loss due to natural disasters	850,000
Loss from Nigerian operations	450,000
Total expenses	6,350,000
Net (loss)/income	(1,950,000)

AUDIT CASE 2

Smarty Pants and Skirts Inc.

Juliet Film is founder and sole owner of a popular daycare, Smarty Pants and Skirts Inc. (SPS). After a long entrepreneurial career, including the successful establishment and sale of two other businesses, Juliet has decided to retire and travel the world.

Before she puts SPS up for sale, Juliet wants to guarantee a high purchase price by ensuring that the company is as attractive as possible to potential buyers. After studying the industry, she learned that a purchase price is usually determined using the capitalized income approach, and that a multiplier for a business such as SPS would be between three and five.

You, CPA, are a senior staff accountant at Smart & Cradle LLP. Juliet has asked your firm to audit the financial statements for the year ending December 31, 2023, in preparation for the sale.

Bruce Cradle, the partner on the engagement, calls you into his office and explains the following:

> Thank you for helping out. Unfortunately, Marcus Seelam, the junior staff accountant first assigned to it, recently quit. He left some notes behind (see Exhibit II). I haven't reviewed them yet, but think they could be helpful to you. I also have extracts from the financial statements Marcus received.
>
> Juliet finances SPS with her personal savings and has never borrowed from the bank on a long-term basis. To date, Juliet has loaned SPS $200,000 at zero percent interest (but she's expecting to recover the principal).

Accordingly, the financial statements have never been audited (see Exhibit IV for extracts from the financial statements). Please prepare an audit planning memo for the year-end audit and include any relevant procedures that must be completed. You don't need to complete an independent analysis or first-time client engagement analysis, as I already have.

Juliet told us that SPS became a registered subsidized service provider in June 2023. In her view, the business's registered status is its most attractive feature to a potential buyer. To better understand the terms and conditions set out by the government, Juliet provided us with extracts from official documents she has received (see Exhibit III).

You decided to spend several days touring SPS premises (see Exhibit I), reviewing the junior staff accountant's notes and other documentation. It is now January 19, 2024.

EXHIBIT I: NOTES FROM DISCUSSION WITH JULIET FILM

Juliet has a doctorate in early childhood education and appeared very caring about the children's well-being. She introduced you to her team: Maya Simmons, the company's bookkeeper, and five full-time early childhood educators. Maya was hired at the beginning of this fiscal year and is a great addition to the team. Juliet explains that her husband John, a retired engineer, also helps on a part-time basis with looking after the kids, resolving computer issues, and ensuring the safety of such daycare equipment as strollers and toys, among other things. Juliet says, "He's such a fast learner. There's nothing he can't learn quickly and be really good at! I'm so lucky to have him around! Plus, I don't pay John any wages so SPS saves money."

SPS is in high demand and there is a long wait list for one of the 25 spots. Parents of children aged one and a half to five years old can sign up. When a spot opens, the next parent on the waiting list is called. Daycare fees are paid quarterly, four months in advance, and in-person, since only cash or cheques are accepted. Maya marks in the parent's file when the payment was made, how much, and for what time period. She emails the parents their receipts as proof of payment at the end of the year. Maya does not have time to invoice parents for outstanding fees, and these amounts are not tracked in the system. Except for inventory sales, revenue is recognized when payment is received.

SPS recently became a registered subsidized service provider. This means that the government will directly subsidize SPS's operations. Parents meeting certain eligibility criteria pay only 20% of the regular daycare fees, while the government directly funds the remaining 80%. SPS is responsible for ensuring that the eligibility criteria are met. Each month, SPS provides the government with the names and contact information of eligible parents to confirm that their statuses have not changed. The government deposits the total specified amount into SPS's account every May, covering the past 12 months.

Maya is responsible for obtaining documentation supporting parents' eligibility. For example, if a parent applies for the subsidy due to having a low income, Maya will accept a personal letter confirming that their income is no greater than $20,000. Juliet then reviews the documentation and signs the reduced payments form and returns it to Maya. Parents are advised to inform Maya if their circumstances change (for example, if their income should pass the $20,000 benchmark). The families of approximately 70% of the children attending the daycare are eligible for the subsidy.

Maya, a single mother of two, is very hard working. To help her save money on daycare and babysitting expenses, Juliet allows Maya to bring her children to work on days when her relatives are unable to watch them. Since the children stay with Maya during the day and only join the others during outside activities, Juliet is not charging her fees. Maya tries to repay with hard work and sometimes works from home. She requested access to the accounting system and her electronic files from home.

Maya and Juliet can login into the system from home by going to a website and entering the company's name and password. John took a course on how to set up and monitor such access.

EXHIBIT II: NOTES MADE BY MARCUS SEELAM

Lawsuit

Last month, while a child was on the swings, one of the handles broke. The child was hospitalized with multiple injuries. Thankfully, the child has fully recovered, but the parents have filed a lawsuit for $50,000 plus any additional out-of-pocket medical expenses they have incurred since the incident, until the end of fiscal 2025. The parents claim that not only was the equipment unsafe, but that a staff member on duty failed to notice the hurt child until the other children grabbed her attention. I asked Juliet for any documentation describing the incident or the lawyer's letter on the case's status, but she has none. Because there is no supporting documentation, the lawyer believes SPS might lose the lawsuit and suggests seeking a settlement for $30,000. It's not yet clear whether the parents would agree to this amount. I left it up to Juliet's discretion whether to accrue this expense or not.

Toy Sales

While completing her doctorate in early childhood education, Juliet created special toys designed to stimulate brain development in young children. She partnered with a local company to manufacture the toys under the brand name "Smarty," at $20 per unit. Based on Juliet's count, SPS currently has an inventory worth $100,000. Initially, Juliet planned to use the toys only at the daycare, but they became extremely popular when offered at exclusive toy stores, retailing for $40 each. In comparison to the competitors, this is at the higher end of the price range for this type of toy aimed at this age group.

In fiscal 2023, a large international retail chain specializing in low-priced products purchased 7,500 of Juliet's toys for $22 each. The purchase was a major breakthrough for her. The purchaser paid for the toys shortly after receiving them at the end of September. Each toy retails for $30 at the retailer's chain stores, for which SPS will receive an additional commission of $3 for each toy sold. At the end of December, Juliet asked the retailer whether she should plan for future orders, but their management said they currently have no plans for further orders, as sales of the toys have been unexpectedly slow. Sales were below target in October and November (700 per month) and only slightly above target in December (1,000 sold). The retailer has not yet paid the agreed to commission for each toy sold.

Sale of School Bus

In 2022, SPS spent $20,000 for a small school bus with a lift for wheelchairs, intending to expand their services to include special programs for children with disabilities. Due to a lack of demand in the program, Juliet abandoned the idea. She hoped to sell the bus, but a specialist discovered a major problem with the lift and suggested fixing it first. The specialist mentioned that the broken part will be difficult to locate, as it is likely discontinued. I have recommended that SPS write down the bus to fair value.

Intangible Asset

When SPS opened its doors, Juliet realized that there were no staff-training materials. She wanted to ensure that her staff was very motivated. She developed a "training binder" and requires her staff sign a confidentiality agreement not to disclose SPS's training methods. I have recommended removing the asset off the balance sheet, but Juliet sees great value in the product.

EXHIBIT III: EXTRACTS FROM CORRESPONDENCE RECEIVED FROM THE PROVINCIAL GOVERNMENT

Dear Ms. Film,

It is our pleasure to announce that Smarty Pants and Skirts Inc. (SPS) has been approved as a registered subsidized service provider with the Province. SPS must meet the conditions outlined below at all times. If the conditions are not met, SPS may lose its registration status and will not be eligible to reapply for five years. Your status is effective immediately for the duration of the next three years at which time the eligibility will be re-evaluated.

- SPS will receive subsidies equal to 80% of regular fees charged by SPS to supplement payments from "parents in need." An individual meets the criteria if they are not able to obtain full-time employment due to disability, have been unemployed for at least the last six months, or do not have the financial resources to obtain childcare services as their total household income is below $20,000.
- Eligible parents must pay 20% of the regular daycare fees, and the remaining 80% will be paid by the government.
- The teacher-to-child ratio cannot exceed 1-to-5 at any time.
- SPS is to act in good faith on behalf of the Ministry and ensure that no parent who has not met the eligibility criteria is considered eligible for the reduced rate.
- A qualified technician must inspect the daycare's strollers, toys, and other equipment on a quarterly basis. If an incident occurs at the daycare, a log of all incidents, including falls, injuries, and thefts must be maintained and made available to Ministry staff upon request.
- SPS is fully responsible for ensuring that all personal and private information is kept confidential at all times.

We appreciate your organization's contributions and look forward to working with you.

Regards,
Tom Flank
Subsidies and Payments Analyst

EXHIBIT IV: EXTRACTS FROM SPS FINANCIAL STATEMENTS

Smarty Pants and Skirts Inc.

Income Statement

For the Year Ended December 31, 2023

	(unaudited)
Childcare services	$ 360,956
Government subsidy for childcare services	279,431
Sale of "Smarty" toys	347,500
Expenses	
Amortization	$ 57,000
Advertising	4,587
Bank charges	1,889
Insurance	12,909
Loss on disposal of equipment	7,000
Office supplies and miscellaneous	27,938
Program supplies	36,807
Rent	72,000
Repairs and maintenance	39,820
Telephone	5,899
Utilities	8,348
Wages	543,338
Income before income taxes	$ 170,352
Income taxes	51,106
Net income	$ 119,246

AUDIT CASE 3

Sweet Tooth Ltd.

Andrew and Abigail Worthstock are majority shareholders of Sweet Tooth Ltd. (STL), a retailer of candy, nuts, dried fruits, and other confectionery food items. STL has store locations across Canada and are famous for the high quality and variety of their offerings. The secret to STL's success is their network of agents stationed around the world who actively search for the best in confectionary foods. Both Andrew, CEO, and Abigail, chair of the board, are heavily involved in the business.

The Worthstocks are thinking of taking the company public next year and therefore want STL to follow accounting standards suitable for public companies going forward. STL recently hired Cavity & Jones LLP to audit the company's year-end financial statements. You, a CPA working for Cavity & Jones LLP, are a senior auditor on the engagement and you just met with partner Taylor Cavity regarding the assignment. Ms. Cavity explains the following:

> Given that STL's year-end is December 31 and today is December 8, we should start preparing immediately. Please complete the client acceptance procedure for the audit cycle and I will draft the engagement letter. This won't take you long, so I would like you to draft a planning memo as well. Include in your memo a discussion of the risk of material misstatement, approach, and materiality.

As you are aware, STL was previously audited by a small firm, List & Lee LLP. The Worthstocks told me that their children and Ms. Lee's were quarrelling at school, which was causing problems. In addition, our firm is much larger than Ms. Lee's, so the Worthstocks want to ensure they switch auditors in preparation of the company going public. We are very happy to have STL as our client regardless of their reasons for switching to us. Even though we are not a large audit firm, we believe they are a great client for us. In fact, STL promises to become one of our major clients and will account for a big portion of our revenues, especially if they succeed with their expansion plans and going public.

I have assigned one staff member, yourself, and a manager to the engagement. This is a bigger team than our smaller engagements, so I am confident you will have no issues completing the audit by January 15, 2024. I want to make sure that the client is impressed with the quality of our work as well as our promptness.

To make sure that we are well prepared, you need to start working on the procedures you will follow during the audit. Please prepare a memo outlining either the substantive procedures and/or control-based testing, depending on which you believe will be more effective for various accounts.

As always, identify any weaknesses in internal controls and provide recommendations. We need to help STL prepare for their public offering in any way we can. Therefore, if you see anything that you believe they need to fix before their IPO, please include it in your report.

You visited STL's premises the same day and spoke with Chief Operating Officer Rose Whiteford (Exhibit I). You also reviewed the minutes from the last senior management meeting (Exhibit II) and discussed operations with the accounting staff (Exhibit III). You were not able to speak with the controller, as she was in training. Fortunately, Rose appeared to be very knowledgeable in accounting as well. She explained that she undertook the role of interim controller after the previous controller retired in July 2023. An extract from the unaudited financial statements is presented in Exhibit IV.

EXHIBIT I: NOTES FROM CONVERSATION WITH ROSE WHITEFORD, STL CHIEF OPERATING OFFICER

General Information

Rose has been with STL since its inception and is a close friend of the Worthstocks. She is passionate about helping the company grow.

Founded in 2018, STL has been steadily growing ever since. The Worthstocks were able to expand rapidly due to a loan (payable on March 1, 2024) from a private investor obtained in 2019. At the time, the investor indicated that he might be willing to stay on board if STL invests heavily in its operations, specifically related to its corporate stores. He believes that businesses should invest in capital assets in order to achieve long-term growth. The Worthstocks mentioned that the investor is willing to maintain his investment as long as he continues to receive 15% in interest payments.

There are 14 STL store locations across the country. Stores offer candies and other confectionaries in bulk bins and sell them by weight. There are also boxed candies available for sale, accounting for approximately 40% of sales. Each store normally employs two staff members and one manager. Employees are given a unique operator username and password, which are required to activate the cash registers.

Goods and Services Acquisition

Most of the expenses necessary in STL's day-to-day operations are incurred through the head office. However, individual stores are allocated a yearly spending budget, which they are to use for the store's individual needs, e.g., repairs, new fridges, etc. If a store incurs an expense, the manager enters the cost, describes the expense and expected life of the asset, and, if applicable, enters the expense directly into the corporate database that keeps track of all capital assets. Managers can view the database and make any additions necessary but are not able to delete records. The vendor's name and address are also entered into the system. Each morning, an accounting clerk pulls the information from the system and reviews it. If no issues are noted, they post the transaction to the general ledger and send a request to the Accounts Payable department for payment (i.e., a cheque is prepared and sent to the vendor). All invoices are kept in-store in case head office requires backup.

Acquisitions at the head office, such as the purchase of a desk lamp or chair, go through the following process: employees fill out the purchase order form and send it to the purchasing clerk. Purchase orders must be approved by the department's manager before they can be processed. The purchasing clerk sources the goods in accordance with company policy (i.e., only approved vendors may be used). Vendors are asked to send their invoices to the purchasing clerk. Once a month, the purchasing clerk sends the accumulated invoices and purchase orders to the AP department for payment. Upon receipt of the goods, a warehouse clerk sends a report to the accounting department to trigger a journal entry to be recorded in the general ledger (Dr. Capital Asset, Cr. AP). When the AP clerk has time, she will match the purchase orders to the receiving reports. The warehouse clerk is responsible for delivering the goods to the contact named on the receiving report. If no contact is indicated, then he will send out a general email describing the asset and hopefully the person who ordered it will pick it up.

On October 30, the accounting manager sent a list of capital assets recorded for each store. Stores then count their capital assets (e.g., cash registers, shelving equipment) on November 30 against the list. Any additions or deletions are to be recorded in the "other comments" box at the bottom of the list and the document is then sent back to the head office.

Inventory Acquisition and Storage

Since candies are sourced from around the world, STL often deals with suppliers using foreign currencies. All purchases are made through the head office. Once the business development representative signs a supplier contract, the supplier then deals directly with head office.

To facilitate business development representatives working abroad, STL holds a bank account in each country to be used for development expenses. STL only has one representative at a time located in each country. Each representative is given a budget of $100,000. A policies and procedures manual is in place that sets out the criteria for an appropriate business development expense. All representatives have direct access to the corporate bank accounts. Due to the local customs in some countries, many of the dealings, from dinner expenses to business introductions, are paid for in cash. If a representative goes overbudget, the COO will contact them directly to discuss the issue.

Since sugar concentration is high in candy, their shelf life is longer than most other foods, although it varies. Dark chocolate candy can last up to two years, gumballs up to eight months, and hard candy can last indefinitely. Shelf life ultimately depends on storage conditions. If stored in an inappropriate environment, candies can deteriorate quite fast.

Until recently, inventory was kept at a warehouse located in the suburbs. However, lately the company has experienced issues with customs agencies in foreign countries. Due to tensions in the region, governments are limiting exports of locally produced groceries, including confectionaries. Some of STL's purchased inventory was held back at customs for two months. Due to concerns about the length of time and conditions of the warehouses in which the goods were being held, STL's local business development representatives were asked to temporarily store the inventory at their homes and the homes of their friends until STL management resolves the issue with the local authorities. Since the inventory was paid for, it is recognized on the financial statements.

Payroll Procedures

Store managers are responsible for staffing their stores. New employees fill out a new employee form, which is sent to head office. Staff information is kept in a personnel file created by the payroll clerk, Mona. Only Mona and the controller may access the employee files, each using a separate password and username to access the system. Generally, store managers will make changes to personnel files (e.g., wage increase) by filling out a change request form. All changes to the electronic personnel files must be approved by the controller before they are processed in the system.

Each store manager creates a weekly schedule that is entered into STL's StoreTime system by 6:00 p.m. every Monday. At 9:00 a.m. on Tuesday, Mona pulls the information from StoreTime and prepares the payroll remittance. Jina, another accounting clerk, is responsible for preparing remittance in accordance with Mona's calculations. Salaries are deposited into employees' accounts each Monday morning. Jina also prepares payroll reconciliations, which must be reviewed by the controller. If an employee does not show up for work because of illness or works extra hours, for example, then the schedule is adjusted and the change will be reflected in the next calculation done by Mona. Store managers determine the rates of pay, which are approved by the controller and entered into the system by Mona. Jina is fully cross-trained on Mona's responsibilities, and when Mona is on vacation, Jina fills in. Jina has her own username and password, which is activated just for the time she is covering for Mona. All employees received a 2% salary increase this year, which was approved by the controller.

EXHIBIT II: EXCERPTS FROM THE LAST SENIOR MANAGEMENT MEETING MINUTES (JUNE 15, 2023)

Present: Andrew Worthstock, Abigail Worthstock, Rose Whiteford, Dustin Cavity, Jeremy James, and Caleb Ball
Regrets: Tana Rise, Candy Whondo, and Chris Kooper

Presentation by Controller Jeremy James

Sales have not been affected by the economic downturn at either the store or the corporate level. STL is, however, experiencing some problems with collection at the corporate level. Jeremy suggested keeping an eye on this trend to see if the allowance for doubtful accounts should be adjusted. Abigail Worthstock said that she believes this trend to be temporary, so no action is required for now.

Jeremy announced his retirement. Management thanked him for his efforts.

Presentation by COO Rose Whiteford

Rose recently completed her MBA degree where she learned that it is critical in today's day and age to empower employees. With this in mind, Rose established a bonus structure for all STL store managers whereby they receive a bonus equivalent to 1% of their store's net income.

The COO proudly announced that sales across the board had increased by 5%, but in one store sales increased by 30%. This is understood as being a definitive indication that the incentive program is working effectively.

Presentation by the Audit Committee (Andrew Worthstock, Abigail Worthstock, and Dustin Cavity)

Abigail announced that STL concluded its association with List & Lee LLP and has contracted Cavity & Jones LLP as the company's new auditor.

EXHIBIT III: NOTES FROM DISCUSSIONS WITH STL ACCOUNTING STAFF

The former controller, Jeremy James, who was with the company since its inception, retired in July. The Worthstocks are still looking for a replacement. In the meantime, their daughter Amy, who recently graduated from university with honours in accounting, has taken on the role as temporary controller. The Worthstocks are considering her as the permanent replacement given her familiarity with her parents' business.

The accounting staff appear knowledgeable about STL's policies and procedures.

The stores' sales data is transmitted automatically at midnight to the head office and is posted to the general ledger. Returns are generally not accepted from customers except in special circumstances (for example, if the customer claims that the candies are in poor quality). At the year-end, the accounting manager randomly reviews sales transaction reports to identify any unusual transactions. She follows up with store managers about any notable issues at the end of December. The accounting manager noted that there were more returns than usual at a couple of stores over the last six months. She noticed that at one store, returns shot up during July and August. During her follow up with the store manager, he said that there must have been a transmission error because he does not remember making any returns. The accounting clerk thought this was a reasonable explanation, did not follow up further, and reversed the return journal entry that had been posted.

The head office also sells to corporate stores to fill up their candy machines. For example, major malls and restaurants buy candies in bulk to give out for free or sell on their premises. Orders are received by the customer service department. Customer service representatives fill an order form with price, quantity, and any applicable volume discounts. The order is then sent to the warehouse manager who enters the order in the system and prepares a shipping document. An available warehouse clerk uses the document to pick the appropriate candies from the warehouse and then packs and ships them. The warehouse clerk signs the order once it is ready. Since candies could be damaged during shipment, the receiver must approve before accepting. Once the goods are shipped, the signed shipping document and order form are sent to the accounts receivable (AR) clerk who bills the purchaser within 24 hours of shipment. The accounting manager will reconcile shipping documents, order forms, and invoices on a sample basis and trace them back to the general ledger.

EXHIBIT IV: STATEMENT OF FINANCIAL POSITION

Sweet Tooth Ltd.

Statement of Financial Position

As of November 30, 2023

	Assets
Current assets	
Cash	$ 549,331
Accounts receivable	314,007
Inventories	1,199,998
Prepaid expenses	87,900
Other	2,888
Land and building	2,700,000
Total Assets	4,854,124
	Liabilities
Current liabilities	
Accounts payable and accrued liabilities	$ 202,929
Long-term loan from private investor	2,000,000
Future income taxes	98,000
Total Liabilities	2,300,929
	Shareholders' Equity
Common shares	$ 500,000
Retained earnings	2,053,195
Total Liabilities and Shareholders' Equity	4,854,124

AUDIT CASE 4

Purple Glasses Inc.

You, CPA, are an internal audit manager at Purple Glasses Inc. (PGI). Today is your first day on the job, having recently made a career switch from an international audit firm.

Your first meeting is with Audit Committee Chairman Simon Cooper. He and his wife, Marta, founded PGI in 1983. After many failed entrepreneurial ventures, they began designing and manufacturing eyeglass frames. Over the next several years, the business grew substantially into a medium-sized manufacturing company. Until recently, PGI's business model was fairly simple: PGI purchased licensing rights for popular brand names, designed fashionable glasses, put the brand logos on the frames, and then sold the products at a substantial premium to individual eyewear stores. These "branded" glasses were sold to retailers only and not to individual consumers.

PGI's new initiative, however, is to sell its own brand of eyewear, "Purple-Glasses," to individual consumers on its website.

Once PGI began selling directly to consumers, Marta and Simon, being dedicated philanthropists, decided to donate to local charities a pair of glasses for each pair sold.

The Coopers have long been thinking of retiring to travel around the world doing charitable work. They finally took the big step in February 2023, officially retiring from their full-time roles as president and chief operations officer. Simon is staying on as board chairman, and Marta also continues to sit on the board. They have no children, but they do have two young nieces and intend to pass PGI on to them when they finish university. In the meantime, the Coopers have hired an experienced businessman to run the company. They employed a headhunter who suggested a suitable candidate—Tristan Farmer. Tristan has extensive experience in the retail industry, previously working in the capacity of chief financial officer at a company that manages online shopping and auction websites in which consumers and businesses sell goods and services. Tristan assumed the position of president on January 30, 2023.

Subsequent to the Coopers' retirement, several long-time employees left the company. Tristan had to urgently hire new personnel, some of whom are working on short- and long-term contracts. The Coopers are very happy with Tristan's work so far. They had heard from their friends, also entrepreneurs, about poor experiences hiring someone to manage their companies on their behalf. Issues such as the manipulation of financial statements because of compensation bonuses and general mismanagement due to a lack of experience seem to have been common. Accordingly, bonuses were purposely omitted in Tristan's contract to discourage financial statement manipulation. The two parties agreed on a flat salary rate for the first two years. The Coopers are pleased with Tristan's leadership despite little guidance and their long absences out of the country. Even though Marta and Simon continue to sit on the board, they are sometimes unable to attend the meetings in person. In those cases, they make every attempt to either phone in or use teleconferencing, which can be difficult as the meetings are usually quite short.

Tristan recently suggested that to cut costs, PGI could obtain a review instead of an audit of financial statements. Before the switch is made, Simon has several questions for you, as he understands you have extensive experience in audit-related work. Simon says the following:

> Given your extensive experience, please explain to the audit committee the specifics of how a review engagement would be planned. I understand that an auditor would consider the company's risk, do a primary assessment of the approach to be taken, and set a materiality threshold, detailing these elements in a review memo. Can you prepare a review memo similar to one prepared by the auditors? Please include any procedures that you think the auditor would conduct as part of the review engagement. Of course, I welcome your opinion as to whether we should switch from audit to review.
>
> I understand from our recently retired controller George Bergeron that hiring an internal auditor has many benefits, such as reducing audit fees because the internal auditor does some of the external auditors' work. If we

don't switch from audit to review, I assume our fees would be lower this year in any case, since you now fulfill the role of internal auditor. Is that true?

Whether or not we make the switch to a review engagement, we will engage the same audit firm in either case.

George has also mentioned that strong internal controls are key to running a successful organization. He believed that our company's internal controls are quite strong. If you disagree, I would like to know what our internal control weaknesses are.

PGI is the only company in the eyewear industry that donates glasses to charitable organizations. Each year we report on our corporate website how many frames we donated (according to our numbers, we have donated 10,000 frames this year). It appears that our competitors are making unfounded allegations that we are not donating as many as we claim. Can our auditors provide at least some assurance over the number reported on our website? What do you think? Tristan says it would be very expensive, but I want your opinion.

Our retirement had an impact on the company. However, I believe it was a smooth transition overall. I hope you feel the same when you get acquainted with the company's history and operations. Anyways, welcome to PGI, I think you will like the corporate culture here. By the way, if you come across any other issues, please let me know as soon as possible. I also welcome your suggestions for improvements and advice about how to deal with issues requiring immediate attention.

Today is April 2, 2024, and you are gathering further information before drafting your report to address Simon's questions.

EXHIBIT I: NOTES FROM THE DISCUSSION WITH TRISTAN FARMER, PRESIDENT OF PGI

Tristan started off the meeting, saying,

> Welcome to PGI. As you know, PGI's controller retired shortly after my arrival. I have not found an appropriate replacement and have assumed the role for now, so the accounting manager is reporting directly to me. It's good experience, allowing me the opportunity to understand the business inside and out and lead more effectively. I think we can make PGI even more profitable than it is right now. In my previous job, I increased profitability through cost cutting and I am planning to do the same here. For example, you will notice from our organizational chart that certain positions are currently vacant, but I am at present not planning to fill them, as we are managing just fine.
>
> As you know, I have already implemented large and positive changes at PGI. Soon after arriving, I established the PGI online store. Starting in March 2023, we began offering affordable glasses, under the PGI brand, for purchase online. I want our customers to think of glasses as an accessory and thus our glasses come in a variety of colours and styles. We realize, however, that our average customer will purchase two frames per year at the most. We hope to increase that number over time. Overall, the PGI brand is targeted at younger customers looking for inexpensive and fashionable eyewear. While PGI glasses are on average $100 and can be purchased on our website, brand name glasses cost on average approximately $300 (only available through retailers, not on our website). We recently renegotiated the licensing agreements with several brands. These new licenses allow us to put certain brand names on glasses that we design and manufacture.

Our meeting was cut short when Tristan's phone rang and he explained that he had to take it, as his real estate agent was calling long distance from the Bahamas and the phone line connection there is intermittent.

EXHIBIT II: NOTES FROM THE DISCUSSION WITH PAT KAPOOR, VICE PRESIDENT OF SALES, E-BUSINESS, AND INFORMATION TECHNOLOGY

Anyone can browse eyewear on PGI's website but in order to make a purchase, customers must become a member, which only takes a couple minutes. Customers select a username (an email address) and password and pay a membership fee of $15. The fee can be paid with any major credit card. Credit card payment is processed automatically and almost instantaneously. Following the payment, customers are sent a confirmation email after which they can proceed with their comprehensive shopping experience. The site allows customers to upload their picture and "try on" glasses virtually. The customer's picture is saved in their account for when they return and purchase more glasses. PGI's website states that each customer must have an individual memberships account, which cannot be shared between users.

Once customers are ready to purchase their glasses, they must enter their prescription and pupillary distance (distance between the centers of the pupils in each eye). This information is found on their eyeglasses prescription provided by an optometrist (eye doctor). The credit card is also kept on file for the customer's convenience for when they return to make future purchases on the website.

After the order is received, it is automatically sent to the manufacturing facility for production. PGI offers a 48-hour delivery guarantee for an additional cost. If the customer chooses this service, their online order is time and date stamped and if the order is not fulfilled within 48 hours, the glasses are free. These orders are marked "Rush" by the internal PGI system and are put in the queue as a priority order.

All the name brand glasses are produced as part of mass production and sold solely to retailers. PGI currently has $600,000 worth of branded inventory in stock. The PGI brand frames are not pre-produced and are manufactured only when a customer makes an order. This is done to ensure utmost flexibility for PGI clients, allowing them to choose their preferred style and colour.

To ensure that the 48-hour delivery guarantee is met, all team members are responsible to work together to meet the deadline on time. The PGI system places the rush orders ahead of other orders in the queue. Each team member has an individual login username and password to access the system. When a team member logs in, the system automatically assigns the next order to the technician and the status is automatically changed to "Done."

If the information is incomplete, the team member will contact the customer to clarify the prescription specifications. Sometimes it is necessary to contact the customer's optometrist. Occasionally, customers upload scanned copies of their prescription instead of a photo, hoping that the PGI technicians will take the information from the prescription instead of entering it in the drop-down windows. When waiting for additional information, the technician will put that order aside and work on the next order in the meantime. All team member access to customer profiles is "read-only," which means they cannot make any changes to the profiles.

PGI has also implemented a new policy, "Perfect – 1 = Refund," which essentially means that if a product is less than perfect and the customer is unsatisfied, it can be refunded.

Pat is particularly excited about PGI's donated frames initiative. She explains the following:

> All PGI employees are very proud of our donation policy. The manager of accounting tracks how many pairs are sold every month and sends a mass email to all employees noting the number of frames to be donated to each charity. We believe that all our employees should participate in the initiative. Employees select a location that they would like to donate to (on a first come, first served basis). We don't like to make a big fuss about it because it's not about the corporate image. We do it because we want to help. One employee makes the donation, which is enough representation from our company. We also encourage employees to make it a surprise visit to avoid any unnecessary "thank you" parties. Charity monies should be going to those in need, not to parties. Employees are encouraged to select charities in or close to the communities where they live. Sometimes even our president would take donation frames and drop them off on his way to another meeting.

Pat gave you her password to access the company's corporate mailbox where stakeholders are welcome to send their complaints and thank yous. The extracts from your review are in Exhibit V.

Pat also says the following:

> Tristan has been great to work with. He really was able achieve a lot during his short time here. He initiated the online store and spent very little time getting the project up and running. It used to take us at least two months, obtaining competitive bids, negotiating prices, checking supplier references,

etc. Tristan hired an experienced firm, Important Technology Ltd. (ITL), which was able to get the website working within three weeks. Of course, some glitches are always expected. However, if we experience any issues accessing customer profiles and requests, they fix the issue remotely or simply extract the necessary information that we are looking for if the repair takes longer than one day. For a team of two people, they are extremely efficient.

Even in a crisis situation, ITL was great to work with. Just a few days ago, a warehouse worker opened a prescription file uploaded by a customer but the file contained a virus. ITL got rid of the virus within a couple of hours.

EXHIBIT III: NOTES FROM THE DISCUSSION WITH GAVIN KIRKPATRICK, BOOKKEEPER

Accounting Manager Tina Seema was too busy to meet with you. Instead, you met with the bookkeeper, Gavin Kirkpatrick. He seemed very friendly and willingly shared all the information you requested. He mentioned that the controller position has been open for about a year. Now Tina, with some help from Tristan, is very busy trying to fulfill the controller's responsibilities. There have been some problems with her login account, so she uses the former controller's login account.

Gavin showed you the accounting software being used. You reviewed a couple of randomly selected transactions for the month of April 2023 (see Exhibit IV).

He also briefly explained his duties to you. He is responsible for posting all transactions in the general ledger (GL), such as all expense reports submitted by employees for processing and recording. Every Monday, Gavin pulls information off the website, recognizing sales made during the past week in the GL. As all payments are made by credit cards, collectability of revenue is not an issue.

Since this occupies all of Gavin's time, Tina now performs several activities that were previously done by other colleagues who left after the Coopers' retirement. For example, she follows up on outstanding receivables and reconciles cash, accounts receivable, accounts payable, and other accounts. Gavin says that even though they both work hard, Tina often has to stay after hours to finish up her work. There are currently three vacant positions in the accounting department.

Gavin also showed you a bank reconciliation for January 2024. You noted that the cash balance as per the bank was $12,160, while the balance as per the GL was $12,560. The immaterial difference was due to a cheque that was deposited but which has not yet been processed. Bank reconciliation was signed by both Tristan and Tina.

The president initiated outsourcing the payroll function to a third party, PayAll Services, a large organization often contracted by medium-sized companies for payroll services. (You are familiar with PayAll Services from your previous audit engagements.)

EXHIBIT IV: EXTRACTS FROM PGI GENERAL LEDGER (PROFIT AND LOSS ACCOUNTS)

Date	Category	Description	Comments	Amount (Debit)	Amount (Credit)	Posted by
April 15, 2023	General and admin. expenses	Dinner with client	Tristan's expense report	$ 319.00		Gavin Kirkpatrick
April 16, 2023	General and admin. expenses	Dinner with client	Tristan's expense report	$ 455.00		Gavin Kirkpatrick
April 17, 2023	General and admin. expenses	Dinner with client	Tristan's expense report	$ 367.00		Gavin Kirkpatrick
April 18, 2023	General and admin. expenses	Dinner with client	Tristan's expense report	$ 127.00		Gavin Kirkpatrick
April 19, 2023	Consultant fees	Weekly fee payment to ITL		$ 20,000.00		Gavin Kirkpatrick
April 19, 2023	Salaries	Cheque #225	Payable to FarmerCo	$ 1,000.00		George Bergeron
April 19, 2023	General and admin. expenses	Laptop and office supplies	Tristan's expense report	$ 12,000.00		Gavin Kirkpatrick
April 19, 2023	Revenue	Invoice #1987			$ 747.00	Gavin Kirkpatrick
April 19, 2023	Revenue	Invoice #8759			$ 570.00	Gavin Kirkpatrick
April 19, 2023	Revenue	Invoice #1676			$ 1,000.00	Gavin Kirkpatrick
April 19, 2023	General and admin. expenses	Payment to FarmerCo	Email from Tristan	$ 500.00		George Bergeron
April 19, 2023	General and admin. expenses	Cheque #226	Payable to Store-Car (corp. vehicle for Tristan)	$ 70,000.00		George Bergeron

EXHIBIT V: EXTRACTS FROM GENERAL MAILBOX (WECARE@PURPLEGLASSES.COM)

Extracts from emails sent to WeCare@PurpleGlasses.com include the following:

> Thank you for your donation of eyeglass frames. The BigGrowth Centre for Learning appreciates your donation, which ensures that our students have access to the quality eyewear they need. It is a privilege for the children that attend our reading groups to wear Purple Glasses. As you know, a large percentage of children in our community do not have an opportunity to purchase eyewear, which negatively impacts their learning experience. Thank you again.

> I ordered two pairs of glasses with different prescriptions for my sons, yet both pairs came with the same prescription. PGI customer service representatives told me that it was because I ordered the glasses using the same account. Thus, one of my sons had two pairs while the other had none. I had to place a rush order but the correct pair didn't arrive for two weeks!

EXHIBIT VI: EXTRACTS FROM THE FINANCIAL STATEMENTS

Purple Glasses Inc.

Statement of Profit and Loss

For the Year Ending February 28th, 2024

Revenue	
Revenue (branded eyewear)	$ 2,899,000
Revenue (online store)	1,910,000
Revenue (memberships)	35,813
Interest on loan to Tristan Farmer	2,000
Expenses	
Materials	$ 277,770
Advertising and promotional expense	176,790
Consultant fees	960,000
Employee salaries	873,487
Sales staff commission	479,809
General and administrative expenses	900,777
License agreements - branding rights	727,887
Amortization	38,798
Net income	$ 411,495

AUDIT CASE 5

Yummy Luxury Inc.

Yummy Luxury Inc. (YLI) runs a small chain of restaurants. Currently, YLI has 10 locations. YLI is a family-owned business, with two cousins, Gregg and Tom Keiko, taking on the primary responsibility for its management. The rest of the family are investors only and while they are not active in the business, they do sit on the board of directors. Yummy Luxury sells fast food "with a twist"—everything is made from organic ingredients, and it offers fast food from all over the world: schnitzel on a bun, mashed potato burger, and shrimp sandwich are popular items. Neither of the cousins were chefs before they started the business 10 years ago, but they have a knack for new food trends. They are also not familiar with accounting and trust their CFO and Tom's wife, Arata Keiko, with the books.

YLI has never been audited and its financial statements have only been reviewed. You, CPA, work at Long & Champ LLP and you have been assigned on the audit of YLI. The partner on the engagement says the following:

> One of the family members who is currently investing in YLI is considering selling his shares. The shareholder agreement stipulates that the existing shareholders have the first opportunity to buy the shares. The share price is determined by a formula specified in the agreement, which takes a portion of the current year's net income, a portion of the balance in the shareholder equity, and a set flat amount.

All parties involved agreed to hire Long & Champ LLP for the audit of the 2023 financial statements. The company's year-end is December 31. Since it's already December 17, I would like you to start preparing an audit planning memo, which includes a discussion of risk of material misstatement, materiality, and approach, as well as procedures. I would like your opinion on which controls are strong at YLI, as well as how they could be tested as part of our audit, and where you see weaknesses in internal controls. For any weaknesses that you identify, I would like you to provide a recommendation so that we can help the client out.

EXHIBIT I: INFORMATION ABOUT THE OPERATION OF YUMMY LUXURY INC.

YLI has 10 bank accounts for general use for each YLI location, one bank account for the general use by head office, and one for payroll. When cash is collected from sales, it is deposited into that location's account. Funds are transferred periodically from the general head office account into the payroll account and from the individual locations' accounts into the head office account. Bank reconciliations are prepared by Marita Claus, YLI's accounting manager. Marita provided you with access to all bank reconciliations done during the year.

All YLI store locations use the Food-IT point-of-sale (POS) software, which is installed on all cash registers. All sales associates have access to the POS system upon entering their employee identification number. Once the customer's order is entered into the system, the total price is automatically calculated, and the price cannot be changed by the sales associate. Any changes to the pricing of menu items is done by the head office automatically overnight and the sales associates are informed of the changes the day before. No issues with price changes have been noted by the employees. All sales data are stored on the cash register's hard drive and sales associates do not have the ability to edit the data. Managers receive a daily report that highlights any processing errors, which are investigated and fixed as needed. However, the errors are minimal and constitute less than 1% of all transactions. Once a week, the data stored on the cash register hard drive is transferred to the head office remotely overnight.

The till can only be opened when a sale is made. If a sales associate makes a mistake, only the sales manager knows the password to void the transaction or open the system without a sale being made.

At the end of each day, salesclerks "close" the cash registers by selecting "end of day close." The system automatically saves data for that day and records balances for the day. A summary of all sales transactions is reconciled and cash transactions are reconciled to the cash in the till. The salesclerk counts the cash and deposits all of the cash (except for $500 that is left in the till to start the next day) to the bank. The salesclerks deposit the funds at a local bank on their way home.

In search of the next perfect menu item, Gregg and Tom went on a long business trip to various countries to select from their best fast food items. The trip costs amounted to $150,000.

YLI received a loan from the Canadian government "in support of full-time employment of Canadians." The loan calls on YLI to hire at least two individuals at each location to work full-time and to provide health benefits to those individuals. The employees must work at YLI for at least two years and receive at least one promotion within that time. Marita mentioned to you in a separate conversation that she heard through the grapevine that it is hard to keep full-time employees working at restaurants, as all the employees tend to want to work part-time while they pursue educational opportunities.

In the beginning of the year, YLI negotiated a firm commitment with a local producer to purchase a specified amount of vegetables for the next two years. If the minimum amount is not reached, YLI would have to pay a penalty fee of $100,000 a year.

In the current fiscal year, YLI entered into an agreement with several large concert halls to operate Yummy Luxury concession stands in their venues. The agreement expires on December 31, 2030. The concert halls pay a license fee to YLI based on a percentage of net food sales. The sales had a slow start but picked up recently.

EXHIBIT II: DISCUSSION WITH GREGG KEIKO ON YLI MATTERS

Gregg welcomes you into this office and says the following:

The slowdown in the Canadian economy did not have a substantial impact on our operations except for one location out west. Our sales slowed down considerably, and we're thinking of closing down the store as it has now became unprofitable. It's a hard decision to make but that's our job—to make tough decisions.

I'm really happy with the way business has been growing in the region though, and we are considering growing further. We have launched a social media advertising campaign with the help of our new social media partner, StartUP Inc. It's an advertising company specializing in social media and other "new age" advertising events. They cost a hefty $100,000 and they wanted all the money up front but, let me tell you, it has paid off! My guess is we have used about half of our prepaid fees.

I heard rumours that the employees are considering forming a union. This would definitely and substantially change our business and increase the costs of operations. I've been avoiding dealing with these rumours but I guess that's something that I have to do eventually.

We're very excited about our new innovation—our customers will be able to place their orders online. All they have to do is to go on our website, fill out the order form, enter their credit card, and the appropriate location will receive their order, which will be ready for the customer when they come to pick it up. We already purchased the system and installed it at a pilot location. I can't wait to inform our board about this initiative. We spent only $1,000,000 on the system. The installation costs, taxes, and training was another $350,000. So, the system is super cheap! Now we just have to install a firewall of some sort—I heard it's important. Anyways, we'll hire some IT experts to make sure our security is top notch. The most important thing is that the customers have already started using our system, and the feedback from the pilot location's store manager is great!

EXHIBIT III: INFORMATION OBTAINED ABOUT ACCOUNTING EVENTS AND TRANSACTIONS AND ACCOUNTING TREATMENTS BEING USED

1. No impairment charges have been taken during the year.
2. All advertising costs associated with StartUP projects have been expensed.
3. The license revenue recorded on the financial statements by YLI is $170,000.
4. Research and development in the amount of $150,000 were capitalized and are shown on the draft statement of financial position. You investigated the journal entry that was booked, which was Dr. Research and Development, Cr. Cash (Note: To record trip expense pertaining to menu development).
5. No finance leases were recorded on the statement of financial position.
6. The full amount of the forgivable loan provided by the government is recorded as revenue.

EXHIBIT IV: NOTES FROM A DISCUSSION WITH WILLIAM SCOTT, ASSISTANT MANAGER

You met with William Scott, an assistant manager at one of YLI's locations (the manager was not available for a discussion). William generally seemed quite satisfied with YLI pay and benefits. He took a lot of pride in his work. He gave you a tour of the premises and it appeared very clean and organized. You noticed that there were not a lot of items in the freezer and William explained that YLI head office makes it a responsibility of each location manager to order inventory. This particular location had a high turnover of managers; some did not order enough inventory and some ordered too much. Inventory is delivered twice per week and anyone in the kitchen can sign off on the delivery. The same supplier has been used for several years and everyone found him to be extremely reliable, so no inventory count is taken when it's received. "It's simply too busy around here and we don't have time for counts, except for an annual count of course," William says.

William offered you any item on the menu to try (compliments of the house). You accepted the offer and found the food delicious. William explains that the success of any restaurant heavily depends on the chef. William says, "We're lucky to have our head chef here! He has travelled all over the world just learning about food and he loves our international approach. Most locations have inexperienced chefs, as far as I know. While the head office provides guidelines on how to prepare each menu item, our chef does not need to look at the precise measurements of each ingredient, he prepares everything from his heart—he feels what the right amount is of each ingredient. Not everyone can do that, you know!"

William confirmed that an annual inventory count is done on January 1 of each year. William gives you a brief overview of the count procedures, which is coming up shortly. The assistant manager and the manager are required to be present at the count. All items are counted; any expired items found during the count are discarded and marked as obsolete on a count sheet, which is later sent to the head office. The count is done twice—first by the assistant manager and then by the manager.

The facility where William works is not owned by YLI but rather leased out from the owner of the plaza where the restaurant is located. You inquired with William whether all locations are leased and not owned by YLI. William said that was most likely the case but he was not sure.

AUDIT CASE 6

Healthy Snack Inc.

HealthySnack Inc. (HSI) imports, produces, and distributes healthy and tasty oatmeal bars. The company was started by Georgia Lucas, who started by importing the bars from Europe into Canada and selling them to private businesses to provide to their employees for free in their common areas and kitchens. Eleven months ago, her sister Althea joined HSI to help expand the business. Althea introduced a new line of made-in-house oat bars. There are now two lines of business—EuroSnack (imported bars) and CanSnack (made in-house).

Until recently, HSI had been financed through the sisters' personal savings. While the sisters are still majority shareholders, a portion of the shares is now owned by family and past and current employees. The sisters also recently obtained a bank loan to finance HSI's rapid expansion. The bank put a debt-to-equity covenant in place of 3:1, which will be re-evaluated annually when the audited financial statements are submitted (due 60 days after year-end). Today is December 16, 2023, and the audit manager has called you into his office and tells you,

> I need you to prepare a planning memo, including a discussion of risk of material misstatement, approach, materiality, and procedures for high-risk accounts. HSI has never been audited. They don't have a full-time bookkeeper, but one of the owners worked in an accounting role for a large company and is quite familiar with basic accounting rules. It's possible that we'll need to

help the client with some journal entries. You can assume the books are a mess, at least that's been my experience with businesses of this size.

I wanted to get a better understanding of the client and familiarize myself with their operations, so I took a look and left some notes in the audit file [see Exhibit I]. There's quite a bit to follow up on. Remember, it was only a quick overview and I wasn't acquainted with their operations at that time. I highlighted some areas of concern, which could end up either low-risk or high-risk items. Could you please look into this? Please meet with the owners and obtain further information to help you out. Don't forget—I am only interested in high-risk items at this point [see Exhibit II].

I believe HSI hired a full-time controller at some point last year. The controller was very experienced and eager to establish strong controls, which he did in some areas of the business. Unfortunately, he had to unexpectedly take a medical leave and has been off work ever since. The sisters say it's unlikely that he's coming back. Having said that, we might be able to rely on some of his controls when performing our testing. Please see if there are any strong controls that we can rely on. If so, discuss their objectives and how we would test them. Aside from these selected areas, I assume we will need to do substantive procedures.

The owners also asked us to identify any weak internal controls so that they can promptly fix them as the business grows.

EXHIBIT I: NOTES PREPARED BY THE AUDIT MANAGER

Analytical procedures are done by the audit manager based on extracts from the financial statements:

Account	Prior Year	Current Year	Manager's Comments
Inventory	$98,947	$387,976	I guess this might make sense given the growing CanSnack business line?
Bad debt expense	$16,839	$17,789	OK as no substantial change?
Interest on long-term debt expense	$0	$6,000	In line with our expectations given no bank loan in the prior year?
Rent expense	$0	$158,000	In line with our expectations given did not rent out the manufacturing facility last year and given no prepaid rent on the F/S in either years?
Repairs and maintenance	$4,302	$17,789	The increase is within our expectations given that manufacturing equipment increased substantially.
Salaries and wages	$145,790	$235,790	I guess this makes sense given the new business line?
Sales	$378,977	$848,989	I guess this makes sense given the growing CanSnack business line?
Net income (after tax)	$78,089	$285,089	

An analysis of trade accounts receivable revealed that they represent unpaid balances. No amount at the year-end was older than 45 days, reflecting an informal target set by the company. HSI's policy is to provide for doubtful accounts by applying a 5% flat rate to outstanding amounts, in accordance with industry practice. Accounts receivable also include demand loans to current directors and past and current employees for share purchases.

EXHIBIT II: NOTES FROM MEETING WITH GEORGIA AND ALTHEA LUCAS

New Business Line

When Althea joined earlier this year, HSI moved to new facilities to accommodate her strategic vision of producing their own oat bars. The new facilities were leased out for five years. The current owner will be retiring in five years and will then either sell the premises to a real estate investor or directly to HSI for a good price. The premises are quite new and if their business goes well, HSI is interested in this opportunity. An operating rent expense is recorded in the financial statements every time a payment is made to the landlord. Payments are made every four months starting March 1, 2023, for the four months following.

HSI also purchased new production equipment. They got a very good deal and bought double what was required to achieve the production volume expected in the start-up stages. Though half of the new equipment is not being used, the sisters expect to use it as soon as demand warrants it. Whereas the equipment being used is amortized over 20 years, the unused equipment is not amortized.

The sisters recently reunited with a long-lost relative, Violet Lucas, a former chef and business owner. Violet is in her late 60s but is still very active. In her youth, she developed a recipe for a sweet tasting but healthy oat bar using only organic and natural ingredients. Her recipe was exactly what the sisters were looking for, so they decided to use it. Violet offered the recipe in exchange for 1,000 HSI shares, and the sisters readily agreed. Thus, the Shareholders' account was credited $1,000, and $1,000 for the recipe was debited.

In addition to Violet's recipe, the sisters wanted to work on producing "organic" bars to expand their product offering. HSI product development staff are currently working on several bars at the same time. Research and development costs are allocated evenly between four different bars that the team is working on. The sisters hope that all four bars will result in commercial success, but they would first need to be tested and approved by the Canada Organic Trade Association. All related costs are currently capitalized under "Research and Development" on the balance sheet.

Description of the Purchasing Cycle for CanSnack and EuroSnack

CanSnack

Jodi Quench, head of manufacturing, was hired when the new business line was launched. Though she has limited experience, she is a trained chef and nutritionist, and these two qualifications make her well-suited for this job. Jodi requested a hefty salary of $90,000, which the sisters were prepared to pay, given her significant expertise.

Due to the company's demands on cash flows, the sisters try to maintain minimum cash tied up in inventory. Ingredients for the oat bars (e.g., oats, sugar, dried fruits) are purchased on an as-needed basis. Georgia and Althea instructed Jodi not to purchase any ingredients until they run out or are very close to running out. When a specific ingredient runs out, Jodi orders more. It can take up to three weeks for the ingredients to arrive at the warehouse and be made available for production. Jodi states that she makes approximately 150 ingredient orders per month, sometimes with multiple orders for the same product.

When an ingredient order is placed using a supplier's website, Jodi prints out a confirmation record and pays right away using a corporate credit card. When an order arrives, Jodi confirms the correct goods have been received (i.e., the correct type of oats) and distributes them as needed. Jodi receives the receipts by email, which she prints out and forwards along with the purchase orders and shipping documents to the accounting department.

Based on the tight controls placed over raw materials, there is minimum raw inventory left at the manufacturing facility when the business closes for the holidays in the second half of December. However, about 20% of regular CanSnack clients pre-order oat bars to arrive at their premises in January. Therefore, some manufactured inventory is kept on HSI premises at the end of December, ready to meet these orders.

All the costs related to raw materials used in production are expensed when incurred, since they are quickly put to use and rarely remain idle for long. Manufacturing staff's wages, including Jodi's, are paid at the end of each month and are expensed at that time.

When Jodi notices that the production process is behind schedule, she hires additional temporary staff to help. Georgia and Althea appreciate that Jodi is so proactive. All temporary staff are to fill out a timesheet showing the hours they worked, which Jodi signs. During the school break in the summer,

Georgia was pleasantly surprised to see Jodi's 19-year-old daughter working on the premises.

EuroSnack

Georgia orders oat bars from European snack manufacturers based on HSI's sales trends over the past five years. She admits to you that CanSnack has been doing much better than expected and will soon surpass EuroSnack in sales. In fact, EuroSnack sales have slowed down since CanSnack products were introduced.

EXHIBIT III: DESCRIPTION OF THE INVENTORY SYSTEM AND RELATED CONTROLS FOR EUROSNACK

The inventory system is automated and fully integrated with other financial accounting systems (e.g., order entry, general ledger). Automatic updates to the inventory records occur at the same time the shipping documents are printed. The shipping documents are prepared automatically from the order forms. The computer system calculates the average cost of inventory items, as HSI uses the weighted average method for recording cost of goods sold.

Inventory reports are printed daily and are reviewed by management, which allows them to monitor what products are low in stock and adjust the production schedule accordingly. Management has also been able to identify slow-moving items using this report and minimize inventory obsolescence by adjusting future production outputs and putting some products on sale.

The warehouse supervisor has a special password, allowing him to access and change inventory information to take into account expired goods, which are written off. An expired goods report is printed monthly and reviewed by management. Over the past year, expired goods have been brought to all-time low levels.

Ahead of the year-end inventory count, HealthySnack prepared the following inventory count instructions, extracts of which have been provided to you:

Count Procedures

[...]

1. Prenumbered count tags will be used. Product stock number, description, and location will be preprinted on the tags. The tags will also include a barcode.

   To record quantities counted, warehouse personnel will use scanning devices to read the barcode and then manually enter the quantity counted into the computer system. Any changes to preprinted information such as a change in location will also be entered manually.
2. Two discrepancy reports will be generated by the system: one identifying differences between quantities counted and perpetual records, and one listing missing count tags. The information will be followed up on, and any changes to inventory records will be authorized by the warehouse supervisor.

[...]

PART FIVE

Advanced Audit Cases

ADVANCED AUDIT CASE 1

Jolly'N'Ice Inc.

Father and son duo Chris and Jess Melty run a small ice cream manufacturing facility. Chris founded Jolly'N'Ice Inc. (JNI) 20 years ago and was this year joined by Jess, who graduated with a business degree five years ago and who has some experience in other industries. JNI distributes ice cream in bulk to retailers (e.g., restaurants, coffee shops) and does not sell directly to consumers. Chris, the CEO, and Jess, the president, are both active in the business and try to share responsibilities. JNI follows accounting standards suitable for private enterprises.

Since its inception, JNI's financial statements have been reviewed by a small local audit firm—Norman LLP. Max Norman is the only partner at the firm. You, CPA, recently left an international audit firm to join Norman LLP, who promised better work-life balance and an opportunity to become a partner. Max put you in charge of the audit. He says, "This is our largest client and given your experience, I would like to entrust you with this year's review engagement. Could you please start by preparing a review planning memo? I have a feeling that the new kid, Jess, will want to go with a big national audit firm next year. We don't want that to happen! Why don't we see if we can provide JNI with some value-added services? For example, maybe you could examine their internal controls and see if there are any weaknesses that could be fixed? Also, please look into their corporate governance—there must be some issues that we could bring to their attention? If we can provide them with some added value and help them as much as we can, I bet they will not want to switch audit firms. Let me know if you need staff to help you out. Otherwise, good luck!"

Today is November 26, 2024, and the company's year-end is December 31, 2024.

EXHIBIT I: NOTES FROM DISCUSSION WITH JESS MELTY

Prior to joining the family business, Jess learned that the per capita consumption of ice cream in Canada is steadily decreasing. In response, he has emphasized growing the business as much as possible and try to beat JNI's competition. While there are currently about 100 Canadian ice cream manufacturers, he believes many of them will not survive this shift in consumer trends. Jess was excited about a new opportunity that appeared this year. A medium-sized hotel chain, Luxus Hotels Inc. (LHI), approached JNI about supplying ice cream for its guest rooms' mini freezers. This would require packaging the ice cream in individual containers, which JNI had not done before (since its ice cream is generally sold in bulk). Jess thought this was a great idea and quickly began its implementation.

To bring the project to fruition, JNI purchased an inventory of containers used to package individual ice cream servings. JNI also upgraded its existing manufacturing equipment by adding a conveyor belt and automatic "arm" to pour the ice cream into each individual container. The containers and equipment were imported from Europe. Duty was 13% of the equipment's $120,000 purchase price. The transportation costs added up to $10,000. An installation team was paid $7,000 to assemble the equipment, but they were unable to successfully complete the job. Jess obtained instructions from the seller in Europe and installed it himself. JNI then hired a specialist for $2,000 who spent a week testing the machine. Jess wants JNI to sue the "installation guys for taking the money and not finishing their job." He took pictures of their failed attempt and has sufficient proof, however he has not yet followed up with his lawyer.

To make space for the conveyor belt, the JNI-owned manufacturing facility had to be extended. A construction crew was hired to take down a portion of the existing wall and extend the facility into the backyard. During this process a major leak in the wall was discovered and the construction company said that JNI was "lucky" the wall was being removed, as it would have needed to be repaired in any case. They charged $20,000 and completed their work on time.

The first shipment of ice cream to LHI was made on November 7. Based on the trial agreement signed between JNI and the hotel chain, the ice cream available for purchase in each hotel room will last three months (the ice cream's approximate expiry date). After this initial trial, LHI will pay JNI $3 per container sold, while the unsold containers will be returned. If the trial is successful, this arrangement will continue into the future with similar contract terms.

Jess is very happy about these developments. He says that the manufacturing facility (which is being amortized over 30 years) was operating at 60% capacity before the LHI deal, and has been boosted to 90% due to the individual ice cream containers. While only about half of the produced ice creams were shipped to LHI, Jess is actively seeking new opportunities in the hospitality industry. He admits that it is rare to have a freezer in guest rooms, so he has not had much luck so far. Jess is approaching grocery stores to sell JNI's single-serving ice creams, but in the meantime the ice cream is stored in JNI's freezers.

The machines have increased their usage from 8 to 11 hours per day. "These metal friends are super durable," Jess says. "With regular maintenance, they will serve for 20–30 years."

Jess's other project has been to create new ice cream flavours. He also hired a team of experts to create a healthy "sugar substitute" for the ice cream. He says, "All current sugar substitutes, while tasting great, are unhealthy. If we hit a breakthrough with this, we can forget about the ice cream business and simply patent this new product. It's a big project and we're doing it in stages, as we don't have enough money for it all at once. I'm not sure how supportive father will be when he finds out how much money we spent, but we're progressing. The team created a first round of products but none were as sweet as sugar. We have to keep going!" Approximately $150,000 has been spent on the project and these costs are currently recorded on the balance sheet.

To finance the new business line, JNI obtained a loan from Maple Bank. The loan will become payable in one year from the date of issuance (October 1, 2024), unless the bank agrees to extend the loan for another year. The bank placed a covenant of 2:1 debt-to-equity ratio (debt is defined as all long-term debt). An annual interest of 6% is charged on the loan and the interest payments are to be made on the first day of each month.

EXHIBIT II: NOTES FROM DISCUSSION WITH CHRIS MELTY

Chris says he has been very fortunate to have extremely competent people sitting on the board of directors. When he started the business 20 years ago, he recruited friends, business colleagues, and mentors to join him on the board. He has no regrets about having spent a lot of time on establishing the board, as these same people (with the exception of just two) are still there. He says,

> The board members are like family now. Even though we meet on average once a quarter, some of them often see each other outside of our meetings. For example, Paolo Henrez, a successful businessman, recently made a donation to board member Yvonne Young's not-for-profit organization, Food-for-Kids Inc. Paolo is a true asset. He singlehandedly formed an audit committee to get deep into our financials (currently, the audit committee is comprised of just Paolo) and reports back to us if he sees any issues. It certainly saves us a lot of time!
>
> I recently recruited another board member—Joyce Nate—who is a nutritionist and also happens to be in the age group that is the fastest growing segment of the market, those aged 60 to 75. She's the first woman on our board, a trend that we definitely plan to continue.
>
> A recent public relations issue drove me to recruit another board member—Raj Mal. Raj is a PR specialist. One of our board member's email was hacked and the hackers stole a document that was emailed to all of us in preparation for a meeting. In that document, we discussed potentially eliminating the use of milk in our production and 'quietly' (i.e., without telling our customers directly) replacing it with powdered milk and vegetable fat. I don't believe there's any legal requirement for us to publicize it, and we believe the taste would be the same. What can I say? The cost of milk is simply too high. Well, we obviously can't make the switch anymore. Now, our clients want to better understand our ingredients and ensure that our ice cream is still 'dairy ice cream.' That is, 'dairy ice cream' must contain a minimum of 5% milk fat and no other type of fat, while regular 'ice cream'

> contains a minimum of 5% of milk and/or vegetable fat (derived from oils such coconut oil, palm oil, etc.).

Chris also explains that the board has been very supportive throughout this "unfortunate incident" and says,

> I explained that it shouldn't be an issue once Raj develops our PR campaign. I'll be personally visiting each of our major clients and this is where you come in. We would like to engage your firm to provide at least some assurance over our ingredients (such as the content of vegetable oil versus milk) and production standards (such as pasteurizing the ice cream at 68.3°F for 30 minutes, homogenizing the ice cream mix, aging the mix for at least four hours, which improves the whipping properties of the mix and freezing the ice cream, which involves incorporating air—up to 50% of the volume of the finished ice cream can be air and premium ice creams such as ours will have less air, i.e., only 20%).

After your meeting, you decide to incorporate a discussion on this potential engagement in your memo to the partner.

Chris also mentioned that the board accepted his placement of Jess in the role of the president. They also approved Jess's salary of $200,000. Upon joining, Raj mentioned that it might be better to have a portion of the salary tied to some performance indicators, and Chris promised to address this at some point in the future. For now, the father and son team are busy incorporating a new accounting system. Unfortunately, the implementation has not been as smooth as they envisioned. After the system's implementation, they went on a week-long family fishing trip, as they had been working very hard. When they returned they realized that the software had incorrectly recognized several pending orders as revenue and marked them as complete. The error was discovered when a customer called in asking about an order that was three days late.

While Chris and Jess were away, a customer that Chris knew to be financially unstable was shipped $100,000 worth of ice cream. Chris has been unable to contact the customer since then.

On October 5, the new accounting system crashed. Chris believes it was caused by hackers who also meddled with shareholders' emails. An automatic backup is done on the 28th of each month, so JNI had all transactions backed up to September 28. The rest of the month-end transactions for September and early October had to be re-entered by the bookkeeper. Chris was quite upset with the bookkeeper for falling behind on her duties. Amongst other things, she is tasked with purchasing ingredients necessary to make ice cream when JNI runs low on supplies. Chris says, "I gave her full authorization to order ingredients and contact suppliers, and I explained to her how much of each ingredient we need. I don't understand what else she needs to do her job!"

Based on these incidents, Chris is considering firing the bookkeeper after the review engagement is complete. He says to you,

> Only Suzie [the bookkeeper] really knows the financial accounting policies and systems around here. You'll definitely need to speak to her as part of your work. Anyways, good chatting with you. I'll see you at the inventory count on December 20. Max might have told you that we are closed from December 20 to January 2. The first day of our closure is inventory count day. Since it happens only once a year, we have a big party in the warehouse when we're finished. You should join! See you then.

ADVANCED AUDIT CASE 2

Gym-for-All Inc.

Gym-for-All Inc. (GAI) is a small public company that specializes in purchasing, refurbishing, and reselling used exercise equipment. Its clients include private customers, community centres in the region, as well as gyms in developing countries.

You, CPA, have just been hired by Engel & Gottlieb LLP and your first engagement is to review the first quarter of GAI's financial statements. Engel & Gottlieb have been auditing GAI for the past five years and consider the company to be an important client. You just received an email from Catrin Engel, the audit partner:

To: CPA
From: Catrin Engel
Date: April 5, 2023

Hello CPA,

As discussed, you've been assigned to the review engagement of GAI for the first quarter of fiscal 2023 (the quarter ended on March 31, 2023). There are a couple things I would like you to complete before our next meeting. First, please prepare a review planning memo that includes a discussion of the engagement's risk, materiality, and approach, as well as any necessary review procedures.

Second, I have a feeling GAI's corporate governance is in a bit of trouble. I would like to help them out by identifying potential issues in corporate governance and providing recommendations. I also want you to identify any weaknesses in internal controls and recommend a way to improve those weaknesses.

I understand that GAI is in the process of acquiring URmove Inc. Since we need to obtain the fair value of assets acquired for accounting purposes, we are hiring a specialist—a valuator to confirm the figures. GAI has kindly recommended a valuator and I know another reliable valuation firm, ValU Inc., which could help us out. ValU employs two professionals who hold Chartered Business Valuation (CBV) designations. Which of these two options do you think we should go with and what steps will we need to take when engaging a specialist?

GAI Chief Operations Officer John Gilbert called yesterday, seeming a bit concerned about the URmove acquisition. He said that the acquisition was set in motion under the previous CEO and John has doubts about the terms and whether the company is actually worth that much. He wonders if we or another audit firm could prepare a report that could provide at least some assurance that this acquisition makes sense for GAI.

EXHIBIT I: EXCERPTS FROM BUSINESS PRESS GATHERED BY YOU, CPA

Date: January 2, 2023 – Press Release

Gym-for-All is set to acquire URmove Inc., a young and growing chain of exercise gyms in Eastern Europe. The purchase price is set at $35 million. The deal is expected to close by the end of the first or beginning of the second quarter of 2023, pending GAI's ability to successfully obtain the remaining regulatory approvals. To finance the acquisition, GAI will be issuing bonds payable on May 1, 2023.

Date: January 15, 2023 – Press Release

On January 2, 2023, it was announced that Gym-for-All CEO Marcel Kalb is leaving the organization. The board of directors will begin a search for a new CEO immediately. An interim CEO, Elsa Keller, has been appointed. Ms. Keller will also continue to hold her permanent role as GAI's Chief Financial Officer.

Date: February 3, 2023 – Interview with Interim CEO, Elsa Keller, Published in a National Newspaper

Interviewer: Ms. Keller, what current trends do you observe in the industry?

Elsa Keller: Home gyms are becoming very popular in Canada. Customers are looking to save time while staying fit and active. Plus, our cold winters do not allow for a lot of outdoor activities unless you like to ski or skate. That's why stationary bikes have always been very popular here. Elliptical machines are also gaining in popularity, as customers are looking for alternatives to treadmills. As you know, our 2022 annual sales across all business lines was $45 million, which resulted in a net profitability of $12 million.

Date: February 23, 2023 – Press Release

Gym-for-All's board has revamped its mission statement: "To be recognized as the world's #1 provider of gym equipment while relentlessly growing shareholders' value."

EXHIBIT II: EXCERPTS FROM NOTES MADE DURING A MEETING WITH GITTA KUHN, ACCOUNTING MANAGER

You meet with accounting manager Gitta Kuhn, who joined GAI on January 15, 2023. Gitta said that the previous accounting manager was fired at the beginning of the year, but she is not sure of the reasons why. She is very grateful to her good friend, Elsa Keller, for giving her this opportunity. Gitta was an accounting clerk at a small gym before joining GAI and is still learning how things are set up, including GAI's accounting policies. She mentioned that there was no opportunity for her to learn from the previous accounting manager and that the accounting staff seemed unaware of how things were done under the manager.

GAI's inventory is organized using the latest version of Microsoft Excel. The previous accounting manager appears to have had good computer skills and created several useful excel files. The inventory manager is responsible for ordering all inventory and negotiating with manufacturers for discounts on bulk purchases. The inventory manager provided us with electronic copies of the following files: "incoming equipment," "refurbished equipment," and "sold equipment." The "total sum" figure showing in the "sold equipment" file matches the cost of goods sold (COGS) figure on the Statement of Profit and Loss.

When inventory is purchased and delivered to the GAI premises, its cost (i.e., the purchase price) is recorded in the "incoming equipment" file. The rest of the expenses such as tax and transportation are recorded in a separate Excel spreadsheet under "other expenses." GAI has five dedicated technicians whose jobs are to refurbish the old equipment. Gitta asks each employee to track how much time they spend refurbishing a piece of equipment and she multiplies that time by the employee's salary and adds it to the cost figure. That number is recorded in the "refurbished equipment" file. Gitta is not sure if that's how the previous manager tracked inventory.

Once the equipment is sold, Gitta moves the cost recorded in the "refurbished equipment" file to the "sold equipment" file. All revenue is recognized when equipment is shipped to customers or when purchased by customers directly from GAI stores. Recently, a large order heading to Europe got lost in transit. The shipping company is unable to locate it and says it was most likely stolen. GAI does not purchase insurance for its shipments, and the shipping company refuses to compensate for the lost equipment. The client has demanded that GAI send a new shipment. Instances such as this were previously rare but have increased over the last several months.

Gitta provided you with the following information on the sales mix of GAI's products:

	Q1 2023	Q1 2022
Treadmills	$2,576,000	$3,091,200
Elliptical equipment	$563,086	$439,207
Indoor bikes	$6,248,589	$5,311,301
Free weights	$1,258,800	$1,233,624

Based on Gitta's recommendations, GAI is currently considering purchasing a new software package that includes a budgeting system, something GAI does not currently have. Currently, expenses are monitored by the CFO and COO and informal budgets are prepared when necessary, but no budget to actual analysis has been made due to the company's successful growth and profitability.

You noted an account called "other reserves" under liabilities in the statement of financial position. The account balance was $4,780,000 and you asked Gitta about it. She is not sure what the account was set up for, as this was done prior to her arrival. Normally, such an account and other similar reserves would be used for legal matters, but Gitta is not aware of any litigation now taking place.

When going through the expense accounts for the current quarter, you note that an expense called "acquisition costs" in the amount of $20 million was recorded in January. Gitta explained that this was before she joined GAI and relates to the acquisition of URmove and includes fees paid to financial advisors and a team of negotiators.

EXHIBIT III: EXCERPTS FROM NOTES MADE DURING A MEETING WITH JOHN GILBERT, CHIEF OPERATING OFFICER

John has been working with GAI since its inception, rising through the ranks from a sales person to the COO. All salespeople, whether selling to corporate clients through the head office or to customers at a store, are on commission. Salespeople are given the opportunity to negotiate special rates for larger, long-term clients. Usually, John will approve these special rates, but he has a couple of salespeople whom he particularly trusts.

John explains that part of his responsibilities is to oversee the IT team. The IT team is responsible for updating GAI's website, updating software applications as needed, and providing day-to-day user support, among other tasks. John is very interested in the IT aspect of the business and says that it is his true passion. While he has no formal education in IT, he regularly attends IT conferences and has taken several relevant courses. John allows the IT staff to update applications as they see fit. As long as John approves these changes, IT staff is not required to meet with the employees who use the application. Employees are informed of the changes by an email from IT staff. If the application change is complex, IT staff will test the application change in advance of informing the rest of the team.

Each salesperson has a laptop, which is required to complete their duties when out of the office connecting with clients. IT staff installed software in each company laptop that allows them to remotely connect to each machine to fix any issues as necessary.

John and Elsa are the only executives on the board of directors. In response to your inquiry about the board, John responds,

> Our previous CEO was not around much, as he was based out of the Czech Republic, which the board considered an important territory to grow in. After an extensive search and interview process, the board narrowed down the candidates to a CEO of a medium-sized gym chain. He is a very capable man and based locally. If he takes on the role of the CEO at GAI, he will stay on as the CEO of the gym chain, which is a major benefit from our perspective. He's got lots of energy, enthusiasm, and knowledge, and the board is confident he will be great for the job. If he refuses the offer, the board will look abroad for the new CEO. An incentive we want to put in place is stock-based compensation. The board really believes that keeping the

> executive's salary low and allowing them to really earn their paycheque is the way to go. Plus, it looks good to our shareholders since we would provide a new profitability target every quarter.

"It will be a busy year for us," John continues. "Out of a board of seven, three members left when our previous CEO resigned, so we will have to find replacements fast. Elsa has been the interim board chair, since the previous CEO had also performed that role."

Based on the review of GAI's corporate governance policies, any director can nominate a new director to join the board. Three votes are required to approve the new director. All new directors receive a stock-compensation package to ensure that they are dedicated and that their interests remain aligned with the company.

You asked John about the acquisition costs that Gitta could not account for, and he said he did not realize there were any acquisition costs associated with the URmove purchase, remarking that "It's just been so busy around here but I'll look into it for you and give you an answer next week."

ADVANCED AUDIT CASE 3

OrangeFox District Hospital

OrangeFox District Hospital (ODH) is a small hospital founded in 1982 that has recently approached Barley and Pock LLP, where you hold the position of senior auditor. The partner assigned to the engagement, Heath Pock, and you meet with ODH CEO Margaret Chen. ODH's year-end is January 30 and the financial statements are prepared in accordance with the same accounting standards as required for public enterprises.

The hospital received notification from the government that due to budget cuts, one of the four hospitals in the region will be closing down and selected staff and equipment will be moved to another hospital. From casual conversations with the government officials, Margaret understands that the government is planning to identify and close the most underperforming and poorly run hospital.

ODH received a letter from the government that outlines the basis on which the hospitals will be assessed (Exhibit III). Margaret states,

> The government officials followed up this letter with a phone call and explained to me that they would like our auditors to provide at least some assurance that the requirements have been met. What are our options here? Can all the requirements be addressed in one report, or will multiple auditor reports be involved? On top of the regular audit of financial statements that the government also requested, I'm just afraid it will cost ODH too much! The official mentioned that they might visit us to see how things are,

depending on the results reported by the auditors. I'd want to make sure that we address any possible issues before that happens. They seem to be particularly interested in how the hospital is governed, how risk is managed at ODH, and whether there are any weaknesses in internal controls. If you see any issues pertaining to these areas, please let me know.

ODH is run by a board of directors. Margaret explains,

I'll arrange for you to meet with Dr. Mark Kraiger, the chair of the board. Dr. Kraiger has a wealth of knowledge, as he was the first doctor to run our emergency department at the ODH. Even though he is now retired, he leads a very active lifestyle and stays on top of the industry. In fact, we have several prominent industry people on the board. For example, Emma Teasome and Zoey Dickinson, both of whom are influential executives at a pharmaceutical company. Given their level of knowledge and expertise, we are just so lucky to have them on our board! To be honest, a hospital of our size would not be able to retain such high-quality board members given our modest retainer fees.

In addition to Dr. Kraiger, you'll also meet Olive Biglow, our new chief financial officer. The position was open for quite some time, and we are excited to have Olive finally on board. Having recently graduated from a business school with a major in accounting, Olive brings a fresh perspective. Many of our staff have been working for the hospital since inception, so it's great to see the next generation coming in. In fact, quite a few staff members have retired over the years with some leaving for larger hospitals with better compensation packages.

Heath has asked you to prepare an audit planning memo, as well as address the rest of the client's concerns.

EXHIBIT I: DISCUSSION WITH MARGARET CHEN

ODH Operations

ODH is a community hospital. The hospital usually sees a surge in patients during the summertime when people vacation at their cottages. The hospital specializes in small and medium procedures and if the case is complex, the hospital is required to send patients to a bigger hospital. If a patient presents with an urgent case (for example, requiring complex surgery), ODH is required to transfer them using its helicopter (based on the provincial guidelines, this must occur within 15 minutes of a patient's arrival to the emergency room) to a large nearby hospital.

The hospital has 5 full-time doctors and 25 full-time nurses, as well as other health professionals and supporting staff. Some volunteers also work at the hospital and help with a variety of tasks. For example, a large portion of patients in the cottage country are elderly individuals who are susceptible to falls, especially when they are not feeling well. Volunteers help them move around the hospital.

ODH Financing

In addition to a predetermined funding amount to cover overhead costs, the provincial government also provides additional funding for each patient visit. Every time a patient comes into the hospital, the patient's health card is scanned. Depending on what procedure is performed, whether a patient stays overnight or not, etc., the presiding doctor will enter the appropriate codes. Each code corresponds to a different payment amount. This information is then sent to the government via email on a quarterly basis, and the government then deposits the funds into the hospital's account.

Because of ODH's small size and remote location, all doctors receive a flat salary (all five receive the same salary). All nurses also receive flat salary, but they also receive overtime pay if they work beyond their scheduled shifts. Everyone pitches in when necessary, but a lot of times the hospital is very quiet with only a few patients.

Other streams of revenue include donations and miscellaneous revenues, such as rent fees paid by fast food restaurants located on the premises and parking fees. ODH also operates a summer camp on its premises for kids who are rehabilitating after long-term medical issues or physical traumas. For its management efforts, ODH receives a flat fee from another not-for-profit organization, Children's Health Inc. (CHI). Management fees are payable bimonthly. The last payment received from CHI was made in January 2024 for six months ending July 2023.

ODH Patient Tracking

Last fiscal year, ODH invested in a patient-tracking software. Its computers are located throughout the hospital with patients' names and statuses, which makes it easy for doctors to monitor their progress. Nurses can enter notes directly into the system. This system allows for a smooth transition from one shift to the next.

EXHIBIT II: NOTES FROM THE MEETING WITH DR. KRAIGER, CHAIR OF THE BOARD OF DIRECTORS

You have met with the chair of the board and he seemed extremely passionate and enthusiastic. You mentioned that you would like to obtain the meeting minutes but he said that it might take a while, as he will need to contact other board members and combine everyone's minutes. However, he's happy to answer your questions.

In light of the fact that the meeting minutes might take a long time, you have asked for the board's agenda for its next meeting. Dr. Kraiger says, "Our board aims to meet as often as possible, since we have quite a few items on the agenda every time we meet. Here's our agenda for our meeting tomorrow, February 15, 2024. This reminds me—I should double check with my secretary whether she has sent out the agenda, I'll be right back." Dr. Kraiger leaves for a few minutes and you take the time to quickly scan the agenda.

Below are the extracts that you were able to review while Dr. Kraiger was out of the office:

Item #1 – The Chair is to present a short list of legal counsels to be hired by ODH to advise on recently emerged legal matters

Item #4 – Review the vision statement: "To lead a healthy community into the 21st century and beyond" and make changes as necessary

Item #7 – Zoey Dickinson's presentation on new products in the pharmaceutical industry

Item #10 – Review of the CEO's 2023 performance review

Item #15 – Review of the final status report of the results of the 2022 strategic plan

Item #18 – Develop a risk management plan (or discuss whether an outside consultant should be hired to complete the initial plan and the Board can take over from there)

Dr. Kraiger quickly comes back and says, "Good thing I checked! She'll send it now." Your meeting is resumed. Dr. Kraiger turns his attention back to the agenda items for the next day's board meeting:

> We try to meet as often as possible, we do our best to meet every month, and on average our meetings are about three hours long. Sometimes we need to carry over non-urgent items on our agenda to the next meeting. To minimize

costs for the board meetings, we at times will transport those board members that live a ways from here in the ODH helicopter. It's definitely less expensive than having a corporate jet or even paying for air flight tickets!

Our board is full of experts in the field and they each have their own expertise to share during our thorough discussions, so some discussions could take longer than others. We have two retired doctors on board, (excluding myself), three executives in the pharmaceutical industry, three ODH doctors, three ODH nurses, two community members, Ms. Margaret Chen, and Ms. Olive Biglow. Our newest addition to the team is a retired human resources consultant, Bettymarie Rockport. Bettymarie used to work for the provincial government in a human resources management role. She brings a wealth of expertise that we hope will be helpful for us in addressing staff retention issues.

EXHIBIT III: REQUIREMENTS SET OUT BY THE BOARD

Dear Ms. Chen,

As discussed, we would like to ensure that OrangeFox District Hospital complies with the following requirements.

- The average cost per patient for an overnight stay must not exceed $500 per night. The costs include salary and staff wages, and a reasonable portion of overhead and direct costs, such as food and medical supplies, if necessary.
- All records of patient visits must be accurate and kept strictly confidential in accordance with the *Privacy Act*.
- The number of patients per year must not fall below 450.
- The hospital must implement and adhere to the best practices in infection control, medication management, and management and use of medical equipment.

We would like to obtain an independent auditor's report providing some assurance that these requirements have been met over the past five years.

If you have any questions, please do not hesitate to contact us.

Regards,
Autumn Davis
Regional Analyst

EXHIBIT IV: DISCUSSION WITH MS. OLIVE BIGLOW, ODH CHIEF FINANCIAL OFFICER

Inventory

All ODH inventory is centrally purchased by an administrative support staff member, Suzie. Doctors are required to fill out a requisition form for the necessary supplies, such as bandages, protective masks, or medications. Some items, but not all, have expiration dates. Once Suzie receives the requisition form, she orders the inventory from pre-approved suppliers. During the summer (the busiest season at the hospital), Suzie likes to take her vacation, so to ensure that doctors do not run out of supplies in her absence, she orders a couple of extra items. Olive says, "Suzie has been doing this job for years, so she has an intuitive sense of what the hospital needs. I'm learning a lot from her!" The inventory is kept in locked shelving units and all the doctors and nurses have keys. Sometimes two doctors may simultaneously need the same inventory item that has run out, but Olive tells you that this happens rarely according to Suzie.

Legal Matters

Olive explains that dealing with lawsuits filed by unsatisfied patients or their families is part of the industry. For example, this year a lawsuit was filed against ODH by the family of an elderly patient who presented at 11:15 a.m. with symptoms that ODH was not equipped to treat, but who was not transferred to the larger hospital until 2:30 p.m. The patient's family claims that the patient was simply forgotten as a result of shift change at the time, i.e., one doctor finished his shift at 12:00 p.m. and the incoming doctor remained unaware that the patient was waiting to be transferred (because the patient was not going to stay in the hospital, one of the nurses decided not to enter her into the system). Olive explains that, fortunately, the patient ended up recovering shortly after she was transferred by the ODH helicopter to the larger hospital. Because of this, Olive does not believe the lawsuit has any merit, as the patient did not suffer any major complications. Olive was told by the doctor who initially saw the patient that at the time of presentation, the helicopter was not available because it was being used for corporate matters.

Another case that occurred this year involved infection control in which a patient claimed that he became infected while undergoing a very simple and non-invasive procedure in the hospital's emergency room. According to him, he did not see the doctor use instruments from a sealed package, nor did he see the doctor clean the instruments. Olive asked the doctor involved whether he remembers the case, and he could not recall any details but mentioned that he would never do anything like what the patient is describing.

One of the things that Olive would like to implement is mandatory reporting of all out-of-the-ordinary events (e.g., patient falls and medication errors), as soon as they occur. Olive is scheduled to present to the board on this matter in October 2024.

EXHIBIT V: EXTRACTS FROM THE FINANCIAL STATEMENTS

OrangeFox District Hospital

Statement of Financial Position

As of January 30th, 2024

	2024	2023
	$	$
Assets		
Cash	140,589	389,583
Accounts receivable	1,587,987	790,701
Inventories	780,005	1,854,888
Prepaid expenses	48,286	35,896
Capital assets (net of amortization)	2,467,489	1,879,874
Total Assets	**5,024,356**	**4,950,942**
Liabilities		
Bank indebtedness	82,820	58,954
Accounts payable and accrued liabilities	321,894	654,988
Current portion of the long-term debt	50,000	50,000
Long-term debt	4,482,642	4,100,000
Accrued post-retirement benefits	87,000	87,000
Total Liabilities	**5,024,356**	**4,950,942**
Net Assets	**0**	**0**

ADVANCED AUDIT CASE 4

ProMods Inc.

Nolan Gould established ProMods Inc. (PMI) in 1995. PMI is a car modification shop specializing in cosmetic and performance customization. Nolan and his wife, Nora, are sole shareholders, though Nora is not active in the business. Nolan worked many years at a local car manufacturer before quitting to establish PMI. There were several car modification shops across the region at the time, but Nolan realized that there was no single recognized brand.

Nolan retired three years ago, after working hard to expand the ProMods brand to five profitable locations. Although no longer involved in PMI's day-to-day operations, Nolan remains on the board and, as he likes to understand the company from the financial perspective, he also sits on the audit committee.

Each location operates independently under a location manager who usually has two senior mechanics reporting to them. The senior mechanics are responsible for overseeing approximately 10 full-time mechanics.

Each location manager is expected to hire an accountant to arrange the shop's financial statements and, in most cases, to serve as an office manager. PMI's chief financial officer consolidates individual financial statements, which are audited by PIT LLP. The last audit was done for the year ended November 30, 2023. Today is April 17, 2024.

Nolan calls you, CPA, and an independent consultant looking for help with a variety of issues. He says the following:

> CPA, I'm concerned. I can't quite put my finger on it, but I have a feeling things aren't going as smoothly as before. I'm seeing some inconsistencies in the revenues being reported by our various locations. While several locations report better profits than ever, one of my older locations is starting to lag behind!
>
> I've been quite happy with PIT LLP thus far. They were recommended to us by one of our head office employees, Penelope, and I don't regret our choice. However, I was surprised that they didn't raise any red flags with me, especially pertaining to inconsistent performances across our locations. Isn't that part of their responsibilities to us? I'm sure paying them enough to do some diligent work and keep me informed!
>
> In any case, I don't want to switch audit firms. Other firms quoted me a much higher price, so I know I'm getting a great deal on the audit. Still, I would like your help with any matters that are not normally addressed by PIT LLP. First and foremost, are there any grounds whatsoever for me to be concerned about PMI's operations? If you notice anything unusual, would you conduct a preliminary investigation to get to the bottom of it? What kind of procedures could you perform?
>
> Also, I wonder if we need to tighten up some of our internal controls. What do you think? I kept a close eye on the business while I was there, but that's no longer the case anymore.
>
> I'd like you to look closely at the financial results of two of our five locations. I'm particularly concerned about these two locations and want to know whether they are reporting correctly. If you think it's worthwhile, I wouldn't mind getting two separate review reports regarding both locations' financial statements. What kind of procedures would you conduct as part of these reviews if we were to go ahead? This will give me a good idea of whether to proceed or not.

Nolan encouraged you to get familiar with PMI's operations as soon as possible. He also asked you to look out for any other important issues and bring those up in your report as well.

EXHIBIT I: ADDITIONAL NOTES FROM YOUR CONVERSATION WITH NOLAN GOULD

Operations

PMI's business got a boost when the provincial government announced its new program, GetMoving. Through GetMoving, the government assists eligible individuals with long-term disabilities to modify their vehicles. Modifications might include installing hand controls, foot controls, safety devices, and raising or lowering the roof, among many others. ProMods was among the first to register as an approved GetMoving vendor.

Nolan believes that ProMods' success is due to a few key philosophies. First, location managers should have full control over all costs and profits at their location. To this end, each location manager receives a generous bonus of 20% of the net income reported at their location. Secondly, working to ensure low employee turnover, Nolan wants PMI mechanics to establish close relationships with customers, just as they would at a small automotive shop. To achieve this, he established the following lateral increases for all mechanics and supervising mechanics:

Level	Compensation
Level 1 (normally achieved during 2nd year of service)	base salary + base salary x 5%
Level 2 (normally achieved during 3rd year of service)	base salary + base salary x 7%
Level 3 (normally achieved during 4th year of service)	base salary + base salary x 13% + health benefits
Level 4 (normally achieved during 5th year of service)	base salary + base salary x 13% + health benefits + dental benefits
Level 5 (normally achieved during 6th year of service)	base salary + base salary x 17% + health benefits + dental benefits + one free car modification
Level 6 (normally achieved during 7th year of service)	base salary + base salary x 20% + health benefits + dental benefits + one free car modification per year
Level 7 (normally achieved during 8th year of service)	base salary + base salary x 20% + health benefits + dental benefits + one free car modification per year + overtime pay for hours worked above 8 hours per day

Nolan insists that this salary structure is kept consistent across locations. All location managers should regularly conduct performance evaluations and hold employees back from rising to a certain level if their performances are unsatisfactory. Nolan generally discourages holding employees back, unless sufficient documentation can support claims about a mechanic's unsatisfactory performance.

Products and Services – Performance Modifications

Performance modifications include exhaust replacements and computer modifications to improve power and brake enhancements, among others. In order to ensure great customer service, all PMI locations are required to carry a wide variety of parts.

Customers can either purchase the parts they need directly from PMI or bring parts purchased elsewhere. In the latter case, the customer is charged for installation only. Most customers, however, rely on PMI for parts. In these cases, customers are quoted one combined price for both services (installation) and products (parts). All revenue is recognized when the customer makes a payment, which normally happens when the car is picked up after the work is complete. As of January 2023, all customers receive a one-year warranty on the modification services only, not on the parts. No warranty liability has been recognized on the financial statements.

Products and Services – Cosmetic Modifications

Cosmetic modifications include custom paint jobs and electronic modifications, such as stereo and navigation equipment installation.

For example, for a special order that involves repainting a vehicle, PMI's designer will propose several colours and designs for the customer to choose from. After the customer approves, which might take a few rounds back and forth, PMI moves into the production process. Such orders can take up to three weeks from the customer's initial deposit (which must be made before PMI starts any design work) to when the customer picks up their newly painted vehicle. When a deposit is made, revenue is recognized.

PMI owns all its paint schemes and colour designs, which cannot be used by other shops or individuals without PMI's consent. All design and colour information is stored on computers in each location, so that any mechanic or receptionist can give customers a quick idea of what their options are.

EXHIBIT II: NOTES FROM CONVERSATION WITH SENIOR MECHANIC GREG LONGJUMP

The location you are visiting was mentioned by Nolan to be doing unusually well. You are meeting with one of the location's senior mechanics, Greg Longjump. Greg appears talkative and friendly. The manager, Carl Weizen, had to leave the office suddenly to tend to his sick child and was not available for a conversation.

Greg has been with PMI for three years and is happy there. In his office, Greg shows you a picture of his family. He speaks fondly of his children and says that he appreciates the work–life balance that ProMods offers. "It's true that I might earn more if I had my own shop," he says. "But I wouldn't have any time to spend with my family. Once our shift is done at 5:00 p.m., I'm done for the day. I don't have the worries a small shop owner has. It's true that our location manager is quite strict; he held me back at Level 1 last year, but I don't mind. He told me that he still appreciates my hard work and dedication to PMI, so I'm happy."

Greg says that a major challenge, whether running a small shop or a PMI shop, is in obtaining reliable and high-quality parts. He's glad this task falls to Carl. He mentions that Carl receives a steady supply of parts from a distant relative who manufactures car parts in Germany. "Carl's love for expensive high-performing cars is no surprise, it's in his genes," Greg says.

Carl also approves all pricing quoted to customers. For instance, a technician will assess a customer's needs, list the required parts, and estimate the number of hours necessary to complete the job. This information is then provided to Carl who will review it and determine the final price to be charged to the customer.

Pricing for customers using the GetMoving program is different due to tight government regulations. Vendors like PMI are not allowed to mark up the price of parts for GetMoving customers and must sell them at the manufacturer's cost less discounts, if any. Vendors are only permitted to charge for the work performed. However, the service fee mark up cannot exceed 30%. If this rule is violated, the government reserves the right to take PMI off the "approved vendors" list.

To ensure the GetMoving program is as hassle-free as possible, applicant assessment forms are available at all approved vendors, including PMI. PMI must ensure the form is complete. A mechanic fills out an order form listing the modifications and parts required by the customer. The form simply outlines the modifications to be done and the price. The mechanic signs it before PMI sends it to the government's offices, along with the applicant assessment forms. The GetMoving program stipulates its right to audit the vendor, but no audit has been conducted on any PMI locations so far. Once the application is processed, PMI receives a cheque from the government (cheques sent to Carl's location are usually made out to "Good Cars Inc. – c/o Carl Weizen"). Once Carl receives the cheque, work on the car begins.

Greg continues, "Carl usually asks my colleague, Mitchell Smarts, to oversee the GetMoving orders. Mitchell has been here for a long time, and it seems like he and Carl get along. The GetMoving orders have increased over the past year. I'm noticing the orders are getting more elaborate. For two days last week, Mitchell's five mechanics were busy with a single order, lowering a car's floor, installing a new stereo, and repainting it. My team was forced to pick up all the other orders coming into the shop."

Greg finishes your meeting with the following: "You should really talk to Carl. He and Mitchell have been here the longest, so they're the experts. Carl is extremely hard-working and does everything around here, even some accounting! You should also speak to our internal audit group—they might be able to help you. They've never visited our location, but I understand they're involved with operations quite a bit."

EXHIBIT III: NOTES FROM CONVERSATION WITH LOCATION MANAGER JACOB KANSON

Jacob welcomes you to his PMI location.

Even though he tries to stay cheerful during your conversation, his worries are apparent: "Our location has not been doing so well. I'm not sure what's changed, but the shop isn't busy."

Jacob has been taking advantage of this slower period to catch up on his paperwork and organize his parts inventory storeroom. ProMods' auditors do rotational inventory counts (i.e., count the inventory of one location each year) and this year was Jacob's shop's turn. It turned out that his location had to write down inventory worth $50,000, as the count found that inventory was overstated. "To be honest, it doesn't surprise me," he says, sighing. "I normally estimate our remaining inventory at the end of each fiscal year by going over the completed orders and simply deducting what has been used out of the inventory account. Lately, I've noticed that our inventory has been depleting faster than would be expected, judging by our profits."

Jacob continues, "Our regular hours of operation are 8:00 a.m. to 6:00 p.m. I'm usually in from 8:00 a.m. until 4:00 p.m. My supervisors have the keys to the shop, so if I'm not here, they'll open and close up. My guys have been working with me forever. I know them well. I don't normally do any performance evaluations, but if there are issues, I bring it up with them. I pay my technicians 1.5 overtime if they have to stay late at work (to encourage them to work hard) but not the supervisors."

The pricing for all orders, including GetMoving orders, is done in exactly the same manner. That is, the supervisor mechanics work closely with the junior technicians to determine the customer's needs, labour costs, and required parts. All this information is documented on the service order form and then a 30% margin (on the total costs amount) is applied. Jacob set the margin when the shop first opened.

EXHIBIT IV: NOTES FROM CONVERSATION WITH INTERNAL AUDIT MANAGER PENELOPE MOOZ

Penelope's internal audit department consists of her and a junior auditor. At one time, Nolan had promised to allocate a budget to hire more staff, as the department appeared to be overwhelmed with work. It is clear that Penelope believes that she has been unsuccessful in convincing Nolan to expand her department, and she hopes you succeed on her behalf.

She provides you with a list of to-do items maintained by the internal audit department on an ongoing basis. Penelope admits that some of the items have been outstanding for some time because she is too busy to complete them. Here is the list:

- Prepare an audit program and perform relevant procedures for the accounts receivable testing procedures as requested by PIT LLP.
- Prepare monthly reports on profitability by product for the audit committee.
- Assist bookkeepers with booking month-end transactions as required.
- Prepare an audit program and perform relevant procedures for the payroll cycle as requested by PIT LLP.
- Respond to the audit committee's requests and prepare ad hoc reports.
- Review all locations' internal controls and provide recommendations.

This year, Penelope decided to return school to "finally get those letters behind my name." She has been working as an accountant and internal auditor for a long time, but only now did she decide to get her accounting designation.

You ask Penelope if she has any concerns with regards to PMI's operations. She again explains that she is very busy. However, she expresses concern about a significant decrease in the accounts payable balance at Jacob's shop. She is also unsure why the accounts receivable balance at Carl's location has been steadily increasing. You decide to look into those areas when designing your procedures.

ADVANCED AUDIT CASE 5

Tcup Inc.

Tcup Inc. (Tcup) is a specialty retailer of premium loose leaf teas, authentic teawares, and other tea-related merchandise. Its in-store loose leaf tea sales account for 60% of total sales, while merchandise accounts for approximately 30%, and other related merchandise (including fresh-brewed teas) accounts for 10%. Approximately 15% of in-store sales are transacted in cash. Products are offered through company-owned stores in Canada as well as through the company's website. Tcup was founded in 2005 by Jed Babble and his wife Arielle.

You, CPA, recently joined the mid-size audit and consulting firm Patel LLP, which has audited Tcup's financial statements since its inception. Today is April 7, and 2024's first quarter just ended. Firm partner Paul Patel wants you to lead the review engagement of the quarter-end financial statements. "The planning memo is already done," Paul says. "However, I would like you to talk to management and identify any high-risk accounts we should focus on during this quarter-end's engagement. What procedures should we be conducting for the review engagement? Focus only on the high-risk accounts and don't forget that analytical procedures are very important for a review!"

"The quarter-end will be a great opportunity for you to get familiar with the client. You might also want to review our working papers for the 2023 fiscal year-end audit. Have fun and let me know if you come across any issues while preparing your memo."

"Jed and Arielle want to take the company public," Paul adds. "They would like our help in getting the company IPO-ready. Tcup's internal audit (IA) department is not yet operational. While the board sets it up, Jed and Arielle would like us to act as their internal audit function. Since Tcup is still a private corporation, it's OK for us to do so. They'll give you the details."

"Speaking of being IPO-ready, let's look at the company's corporate governance as well. Can we give any helpful advice on corporate governance? Also, since Tcup hasn't had a comprehensive risk management assessment in a long time, please note any relevant risks and provide appropriate mitigating factors."

EXHIBIT I: EXTRACTS FROM THE MEETING MINUTES WITH JED AND ARIELLE BABBLE

Jed and Arielle are happy to meet you and provide more information about the company, realizing you are new to the team. They explain,

> Tcup has developed a strong culture, very distinct from other retail companies. We focus on providing a high level of customer service, demonstrated by our knowledge and love of loose leaf tea and enthusiasm for Tcup products.
>
> Our business is seasonal. A higher portion of net sales is realized during the fourth quarter, due to the impact of the holiday selling season. In general, tea sales are heavily dependent on disposable income. A new tea culture has quickly spread across North America, and we hope it's here to stay. Did you know that Canadian tea consumers have an average of 11 types of tea in their cupboard?
>
> Shipped tea may contain contaminants, like Salmonella, that we are not able to detect. Sometimes we are subject to involuntary product recalls for both our teas and teawares. We build strong relationships with our suppliers, visit their premises, and engage consultants and auditors to do some due diligence work. Once we find a good supplier, we try to stick with them. For example, our two largest suppliers represent 35% and 25%, respectively, of our total inventory purchases. This quarter, one of our smaller suppliers informed us that a glass infuser cup is being recalled. Based on our agreement with the supplier, we are fully reimbursed for the damage. Since we are not going to be "out of pocket," we don't believe we need to book any journal entries. However, this glass infuser cup is a bestseller and we still have many in stock. Customers who bring the cup back will be offered either store credit or a cash refund. If customers paid with store credit or a gift card, they'll be offered store credit. We expect 20% of customers will accept store credit. We must send the infuser cups back to the supplier no earlier than September 30, 2024, and no later than October 30.
>
> Even prior to the recall, we noticed a high-level of returns of this specific infuser cup. However, more unusual is that one of our locations has been receiving a lot of returns in general. It would be great if you could meet with the location manager, Gary Poodle.
>
> An important financial measure in our business is average sales per square foot, as well as comparable store sales (comparing the sales of stores open for at least one year). We have also set out some goals for the year and

hope you can serve as a value-for-money auditor. For now, we're interested in the following:

- anticipating and responding effectively to consumer preferences and consumer and economic trends;
- providing a product offering that generates new and repeat visits to our stores and website;
- obtaining and distributing products efficiently.

Can you provide examples of procedures that a value-for-money auditor, also known as a performance auditor, would conduct to measure how well we are doing in relation to these goals?

Our single distribution centre allows us to realize economies of scale. The products are shipped to the centre by our vendors and then distributed from there to our stores and e-commerce customers. Stores often receive shipments multiple times per week, as inventory shortages would be detrimental to our brand name and customers. The recent decline in fuel prices had a very favourable impact on our bottom line, but as our stores grow, it's becoming harder for the distribution centre to work efficiently.

Unfortunately, one of our largest stores closed in January. It was located in a mall that rapidly lost traffic in 2023. We relocated some employees and are paying $550,000 in severance pay to the rest. The severance pay is being paid out equally over six months, starting January 31, the day the store closed. The lease agreement stipulated that we cannot sublease the store and last month we paid a termination penalty of $600,000.

Customers can return merchandise within 90 days. We do not resell returned teaware for hygienic reasons. We also offer customers regular discounts. Last month we ran an in-store promotion called "Choose your savings," where we took $5 off a $50 order, and $15 off of $100. This was a "whisper" campaign offered only to our loyalty card members when they told an associate they got an email about the promotion. Research shows that customers appreciate exclusive discounts and feeling like they are a part of an "elite" club. The campaign was a success! Gary's store had the largest number of discounted sales, with almost 100% of all sales this month (in comparison to 20% in other stores). Gary always does such a great job!

We're piloting something really fun this quarter: we're going to make tea lattes! We purchased several milk frothers for our larger stores. They are expensive but we're really excited. We already have some recipes patented (received the patent in January 2024). Wouldn't you like an earl grey, maple syrup, or caramel green tea latte?

Please do extensive inventory counts as part of your quarter-end work. Our policy is to have at least one of our stores do an inventory count every quarter. Gary's store did the most recent count. They found they had more inventory according to their inventory system than they actually counted. We asked Gary to write off the "excess" inventory, but we want to know if it's the same at other locations.

Before meeting with Gary and preparing your memo, you review the auditors' notes on the year-end audit, as well as some additional information.

EXHIBIT II: EXTRACT FROM 2023 TCUP AUDIT FILE

Memo
To: Tcup Audit File – 2023
Date: December 30, 2023
From: Joe Berke
Re: Minutes from the meeting with Gary Poodle

Gary Poodle started at Tcup when its first store opened. He worked his way up to store manager. He recently applied for the position of corporate buyer but did not get the promotion. The position involved a lot of travel, which is something that appealed to Gary.

Some years ago, Gary tried completing his CPA designation and failed. He decided accounting was not really for him and got the job at Tcup. He went on to complete an online MBA degree and helped Tcup set up its accounting policies. Gary still does all the paperwork and accounting at the store level, just as any other manager would.

Gary says, "To get something done, you need to do it yourself, isn't that so in your line of work as well? That's why I take care of the important things such as handling cash and ringing in sales, handling returns or complaints, and hiring and firing personnel." Gary complained about the store's high turnover, but he puts in long hours to keep the store running (the assistant manager position is vacant).

EXHIBIT III: EXTRACT FROM 2023 TCUP AUDIT FILE (INVENTORY SECTION)

Memo
To: Tcup Audit File – 2023
Date: December 30, 2023
From: Joe Berke
Re: Inventory count

Inventory procedures followed by Tcup staff (see D112).

Patel LLP visited the main warehouse and randomly selected a sample of 20 items for the "sheet-to-floor" testing. The items are listed as follows:

Inventory item	**Found (✓) / not found (✘)**
Earl grey tea (1 kilogram)	✓
Rooibos tea (1 kilogram)	✓
White tea (1 kilogram)	✓
White tea (1 kilogram)	✓
White tea (1 kilogram)	✓
Glass cup infusers (10 cups per package)	✓
Earl grey tea (1 kilogram)	✘
Tea pots (2 tea pots)	✓
Jasmine dragon tea (1 kilogram)	✓
Samurai chai tea (1 kilogram)	✓
White tea (1 kilogram)	✓
Citrus mint tea (1 kilogram)	✓
Caramel almond tea (1 kilogram)	✓
Slimful chocolate tea (1 kilogram)	✓
Bamboo toolkit tea (10 per package)	✓
Jasmine dragon tea (1 kilogram)	✓
Samurai chai tea (1 kilogram)	✓
White tea (1 kilogram)	✓
Citrus mint tea (1 kilogram)	✘
Caramel almond tea (1 kilogram)	✓

Conclusion: Items not found (indicated above as **✘**) are below the materiality threshold and below the performance materiality threshold, therefore no further action is required.

EXHIBIT IV: EXCERPTS FROM TCUP'S FINANCIAL STATEMENTS

	For the Quarter Ended March 31, 2024 *(in thousands)*	**For the Quarter Ended December 31, 2023** *(in thousands)*
Sales	$ 7,965	$ 6,177
Cost of sales	3,723	2,684
Gross profit	4,242	3,493
Selling, general, and administration expenses	4,676	2,953
Results from operating activities	(434)	541
Finance costs	176	128
Income (loss) before income taxes	(610)	413
Provision for income tax (recovery)	(108)	171
Net income (loss)	(502)	242

EXHIBIT V: EXCERPTS FROM THE PERMANENT AUDIT FILE

Additional Information on the Board of Directors

Director Name	Classification	Ownership*	Committees			Years on Board
			Audit	Compensation	Nominating	
Robert Zinberg – Chairman	Independent	yes				2
Mitchum Fenn	Independent	yes	x	x	x	5
Katie Billings	Independent	yes				12
Gregg Hack	Independent	yes	x	x	x	7
Jed Babble	Not independent	52%				6
Jim Leahy	Independent	yes		x	x	15
Wayne Ortega	Independent	yes	x			5

* Percentages displayed for ownership above 5%, when available

Director Name	Attended at least 75% of meetings	Additional Company Directorship
Robert Zinberg – Chairman	Yes	None
Mitchum Fenn	Yes	Fenn Inc.*
Katie Billings	Yes	LeaseMe Corp; Electro Inc.
Gregg Hack	Yes	GreenRocket Inc.*, Swiss Choc Inc., PopUp Inc.
Jed Babble	Yes	Fenn Inc.
Jim Leahy	Yes	GoodCo Inc.,* Pure Inc., Dot Inc.
Wayne Ortega	Yes	GrezInc., Gem Inc.

* The director is also an active C-suite officer of the corporation

CEO Compensation Breakdown – Fiscal 2023		
Fixed	Cash - salary	$120,000
	Cash - benefits	$23,000
	Total	$143,000
Performance-based	Cash	$1,800,000
	Non-cash	$0
	Total	$1,800,000

EXHIBIT VI: EXCERPTS FROM THE BOARD SELF-ASSESSMENT SURVEY

Below are excerpts from the anonymous survey results completed by the board members. (All figures are rounded.)

Survey Question #		Strongly Disagree	Disagree	Neutral	Agree	Strongly Agree
1.2	There is an effective process for measuring the CEO's performance	14%	29%	14%		43%
1.6	The board receives acceptable explanations for significant financial and quality performance variances		29%	29%		43%
1.9	The board is adequately involved in the process of developing strategic plans	29%	29%		29%	14%
2.3	Committee reports are effective in providing the necessary information to the board	29%		29%		43%

PART SIX

Financial Accounting with Finance Concepts Cases

FINANCIAL ACCOUNTING WITH FINANCE CONCEPTS CASE 1

Carretera Travels Inc.

You, CPA, are an experienced consultant at Sanchez Garcia Consultants LLP. Bill Sanchez, a partner at the firm, approaches you and says, "Unfortunately, the senior consultant previously assigned to the Carretera Travels Inc. (Carretera or CTI) file took leave for personal reasons. I want you to take over. The company will soon release its first quarter financial statements and that's what you'll be working on. Your first task is to review the company's financial accounting policies and determine if any changes are required."

Today is April 14 and you are starting your work. The quarter ended on March 31, 2023.

Diego Scotty founded Carretera in 1978 and it has since passed through his family. In 1998, Diego's children took the company public and at the end of fiscal 2022, Diego's grandson Maurice Scotty became CEO. Maurice graduated with a business degree from a local university before joining Carretera as the director of operations two years ago. The family still owns 30% of the business and the rest of the shares are held by family and friends. Currently, Carretera has a small bank loan of $50,000 at an annual interest rate of 7%. The company's tax rate is 25%.

Carretera conducts three businesses:

- Commercial services (Carretera-Complete®) – Carretera offers commercial customers a comprehensive all-in-one transportation solution for their business, providing the opportunity to fully outsource delivery services to a third party. The service provides the vehicles, maintenance, and administrative services (including hiring drivers, routing, and scheduling).

- Commercial rental (Carretera-Rent®) – Carretera targets commercial customers looking to supplement their private fleet of vehicles on a short-term basis (from one day to one year), due to seasonal increases in their business or some special projects.
- Used vehicles – Carretera sells used vehicles at its company-owned retail centers throughout North America or through their website. Before a vehicle is put up for sale, it undergoes a detailed inspection. The company makes every effort to sell its used vehicles at prices above book value.

During the worst of the 2008 recession, Carretera was barely breaking even, and during the recent economic crisis, the business was on the verge of bankruptcy. The business slowly picked up again, and Carretera returned to profitability; however, Maurice is very concerned with how closely tied profits are to the broader economic conditions. He wants you to provide a high-level analysis on the company's economic dependency and discuss strategies on how the business can become less affected by fluctuations in the North American economy.

Carretera is looking to invest in 10 high-powered car washers. Each washer will cost $13,000 upfront and will be used to clean all used vehicles prior to sale, which Carretera expects will increase their selling price by 10%. Carretera currently earns $200,000 per year from the sale of used vehicles. Maurice expects the washers to have a useful life of five years after which they will need to be replaced due to the significant wear and tear expected from daily use. The assets will be depreciated on a straight-line basis. The high-powered cleaners will also be used regularly to clean rental cars, reducing the time spent cleaning vehicles by 20 minutes per garage and repair employee. Maurice expects this to free up productive capacity, enabling garage and repair employees to act as part-time sales staff by using this time to call commercial customers and sell Carretera-Complete® and Carretera-Rent® services. Maurice recognizes that sales and marketing training will be required to get these employees familiar with how best to sell these services. He found a sales consulting firm offering an annual one-week seminar for $30,000 for all Carretera's 65 garage and repair employees. The negotiated price of the course is anticipated to increase by $5,000 annually to budget for increases in Carretera's workforce and inflation. It is expected that the training and sales efforts will generate an additional \$50,000 of revenue in the first year, increasing by 15% each subsequent year. Maurice wants you to help him decide if he should go forward with purchasing the high-powered cleaners and determine how long it will take to recover their initial cost.

EXHIBIT I: DISCUSSION WITH ANTONIA LOPEZ, DIRECTOR OF CORPORATE ACCOUNTING

Antonia was recently promoted to the position of Director of Corporate Accounting from her previous job as accounting clerk of the Corporate Purchases and Payroll Department. She is very excited about her new role and all the changes that are taking place at Carretera under the new CEO, including an overall refocusing on increased profitability. The CEO was extremely happy to see crude oil prices remain low during the first quarter, as this would positively impact the company's bottom line. Management also took proactive measures. For example, Antonia says that Carretera has adopted a new policy for revenue recognition for its commercial services (i.e., Carretera-Complete®). Customers are normally required to pay for services six months in advance (or two quarters ahead). Senior management asked Antonia to recognize the revenue as soon as the payment is made. Antonia objected to this policy, saying that she can only recognize revenue equivalent to one quarter or three months, since CTI reports financial results on a quarterly basis. Now, for example, if a customer pays $20,000 for six months of commercial services, Antonia will immediately recognize $10,000 as revenue while the remaining $10,000 is recognized exactly three months later.

Commercial rental services (i.e., Carretera-Rent®) are provided on credit. Revenue is recognized when the vehicle is returned to Carretera's garage after the rental period. Many of Carretera's commercial rental customers are repeat clients, so the company feels comfortable extending credit. Payments are made by cheque or wire transfer. Antonia noticed that customers are increasingly paying later than usual, which has resulted in a greater number of accounts going over 120 days. Antonia will soon begin following up on the outstanding balances to determine whether Carretera should be expecting payments. The estimated allowance for doubtful accounts has not recently been revised and is kept at a steady 3% of credit sales.

All vehicles have been historically amortized over eight years; however, at a meeting with the senior management team in late March, Antonia was told to amortize two-thirds of the fleet's vehicles over 10 rather than 8 years going forward. Management explained that two-thirds of the fleet had received a major retrofit, which they believe will extend the vehicles' lives from 8 to 10 years. When Antonia asked for details about the retrofit, management said the vehicles received thorough technical inspections and were painted in Carretera's corporate colours. Only one vehicle was found to have an issue, with its accelerator, which was addressed.

Unfortunately, a large customer, FruitsVeggies Inc., recently filed a lawsuit against Carretera for $1,000,000. FruitsVeggies had contracted out Carretera-Complete® to deliver products to its customers. They claim that Carretera drivers failed to deliver the products on time and as a result the fruits and vegetables went bad. FruitsVeggies say that because these low-quality products were delivered to their customers, they now have to give discounts to patch up relations with them. Carretera's lawyer says that there is about a 60% chance that Carretera would be found guilty if the case went to court. However, the lawyer believes that $1,000,000 is excessive and unrealistic. Therefore, the lawyer advised management to consider settling the case before it goes to court. Either way, it could take several years until the case is resolved.

Carretera management recognizes that Carretera-Complete®'s key to success is its ability to plan routes, track vehicles, and communicate with drivers effectively and efficiently. In January 2023, Carretera implemented new software that replaced its six-year-old, out-of-date software. The software required some specialty hardware upgrades as well. The software was tailor-made for Carretera by a third party, App Inc., for $100,000. The asset is currently not amortized.

EXHIBIT II: DISCUSSION WITH JUNIOR CONSULTANT AT SANCHEZ GARCIA

Amelio, a junior consultant, mentioned that Antonia was appointed to her role just as the consulting engagement started. Antonia told Amelio that she reviewed all of the outstanding accounts receivable balances upon taking up her position. She noticed a familiar name—FelizPro Inc.—and decided to give the owner a call. FelizPro is a regular customer of Carretera-Rent®. FelizPro's owner was surprised to learn that there were any accounts receivable outstanding, as six weeks earlier he had personally signed a cheque to Carretera for $9,465.

Antonia mentioned that she inquired with the accounts receivable clerk, Zaina, who said it must have been a computer glitch. The next day, Antonia noticed a credit of $15,889 applied to FelizPro's account. When she looked for other outstanding accounts receivable, she found that $15,889 was owed by another company—CremeEgg Inc.—whose account was still showing an outstanding balance. Antonia has simply not had the time to review any other growing accounts receivable. In addition, she trusts Zaina, who is her long-time colleague and friend.

FINANCIAL ACCOUNTING WITH FINANCE CONCEPTS CASE 2

GreenSmart Inc.

You, CPA, recently joined the offices of Carter LLP. Your boss, Desmond Carter, calls you into his office and says, "As you know, recently a firm approached us that specializes in buying out underperforming companies that could be turned around. They are intrigued by GreenSmart Inc. (GSI) and would like us to do some preliminary research on the company. GSI has allowed us to review their financial data for the first quarter of 2023 and inform our client of any findings. The company has not recorded some of the transactions that took place in the first quarter of 2023. Your task is to explain the impact of these transactions on the financial statements. Our client is aware that the company is not doing well, but they are unsure as to what extent. Please make sure to discuss in your memo whether you believe GSI is a going concern."

GSI is an eco-friendly chemical manufacturer specializing in a variety of products such as paint and glue. GSI sells to individual retailers as well as to big companies that use these products in their manufacturing processes. GSI is a public company.

Today is April 16, 2023, and you immediately commence your work.

EXHIBIT I: INFORMATION GATHERED BY CPA

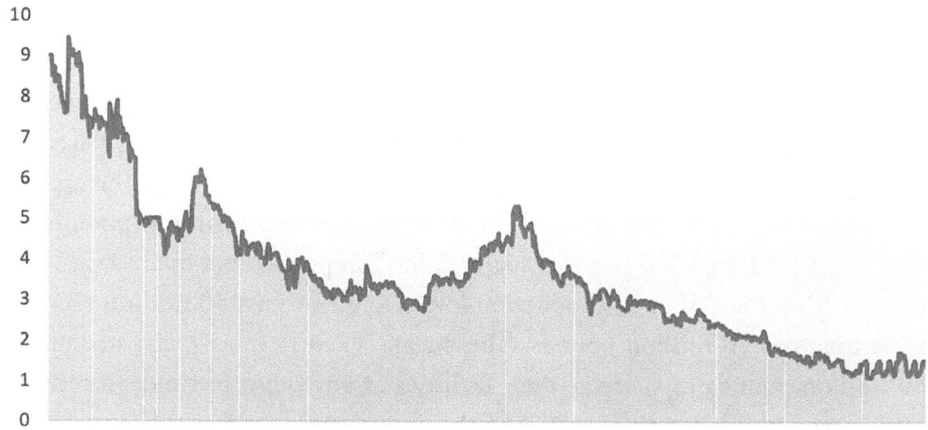

The chart above represents GSI's trading price since going public in 2018 to today's date. Connor Lax, the company's founder, had previously worked at a large manufacturing firm that produced glue and paint that were harmful to the environment. He left and decided to dedicate his life to "making the world a greener place."

EXHIBIT II: INFORMATION GATHERED BY CPA FROM CONVERSATIONS WITH GSI STAFF

In 2021, as the economy began to slowly recover from the market downturn of 2020, GSI's small facility reached its capacity and Connor decided against investing in fixed assets. Instead, GSI entered into a manufacturing partnership agreement with Factura Inc. to help produce GSI products. The agreement stipulates that GSI is committed to producing 50 million pounds of glue (dedicated capacity) per year (or 12.5 million pounds per quarter) at Factura's facilities and that its production levels could surpass 50 million pounds to as much as 70 million pounds. This means Factura must guarantee up to 50 million pounds capacity at their facilities at any point in time. In return, GSI is responsible for paying 80% of the annual contract fee to Factura even if no production takes place at Factura's facilities. During the first quarter of 2023, GSI requested Factura to produce 7 million pounds of glue.

At the end of the 2022 fiscal year, Connor called together the executive team and expressed his disbelief at how low the stock price had fallen. He stated that the mission of the next fiscal year would be to increase the share price. He said, "I'm confident that the market is undervaluing our stock. I think we should consider buying stock back." It was decided by senior management and approved by the Board of Directors that 60,000 shares would be purchased back for $3 per share on March 31, 2023. At that time, the average price of shares issued to date was $8.10.

GSI continues to undertake research and development activities on a regular basis. In January 2023, GSI introduced one such newly created product into commercial production—EcoMax, the main commercial application of which is to be a glue or "binder" in the manufacture of plywood used in the construction of houses. EcoMax is a bio-based product made using material from natural sources, which means it offers a reduced carbon footprint. Once commercial sales commence, EcoMax will sell for $2 per pound. It costs GSI $0.50 to manufacturer one pound of EcoMax. To market EcoMax, GSI shipped "samples" to various manufacturers. Manufacturers choosing to become customers will be charged for these samples on their first invoice. Manufacturers that do not become customers can keep the samples for free. Shipments of all samples have been recognized into revenue. In general, revenue is recognized upon shipment.

Every quarter (including the current quarter), the executives receive stock options in addition to their normal compensation. The exercise price of the stock options issued this quarter is $12 per share and the expiry date is March 31, 2024.

GSI received trademark protection for EcoMax in Canada in January 2023 and has also applied for trademark protection in the United States.

A September 2022 industry report projected that the glue industry would grow by 7% by 2025.

EXHIBIT III: MEETING NOTES FROM DISCUSSION WITH ADALYN NORTEGA, ACCOUNTING MANAGER, AND CONNOR LAX

Approximately 75% of all revenues come from four large manufacturing customers. The rest of the revenue comes from retailers and smaller manufacturing companies. One of GSI's main customers, Calendo Inc., which accounts for 15% of GSI sales, indefinitely halted production at one of its two facilities in Eastern Europe. The manufacturer had recently received a shipment worth $1,500,000, which they bought on credit. Connor is extremely upset about this, and he personally called Calendo's CEO and said that if they do not pay the outstanding amount, GSI will demand all of its shipped products back. The CEO replied that about 60% of the products had already been used, but that he would be OK with shipping the remainder back. The CEO told Connor in confidence that the company is trying to avert bankruptcy but if it happens, all of the corporation's assets would be seized by creditors, including remaining inventory.

Despite GSI's operational difficulties, cash flow has not been an issue as they had accumulated a lot of cash during the previous years when the company was profitable and also from their financing arrangements.

Given that GSI's growth has recently stalled, Connor decided to make some investments. He knows that if a company makes a "good" investment (e.g., investing in a company with substantial growth or investing in a strategic growth partner), the share price of the "parent" company will increase. In addition, Connor likes to play on the open market and invests his personal savings regularly. In February 2023, GSI purchased common shares issued by a public company, Plantations Inc., one of the largest producers of corn, which is the main component that is used by GSI in its production process. The shares purchased by GSI represent 0.2% of the total outstanding shares of Plantations. When asked about the investment, Connor says,

> I bought the shares for two reasons. One, the stock price has been increasing every day since the CEO made a public statement that growth would be 150% next quarter and up to 300% next year. What could be better? Two, I'm going to the annual meeting next month and I've already spoken to the CEO once on the phone. GSI is a small- to medium-sized company but

Plantations is a giant, and now that we have equity, I think Plantations will be very interested in building a relationship with us. Maybe I can convince them to talk to their other investors and sell to us for a discount. In either case, I'm confident that this is either a great investment that will triple our money or a good strategic move on my part.

EXHIBIT IV: SELECT FINANCIAL INFORMATION – BALANCE SHEET

GreenSmart Inc.

Balance Sheet

As of March 31, 2022 and 2023

	2023	2022
Assets		
Cash	$ 23,822,985	30,453,479
Accounts receivable	1,329,076	2,045,896
Inventories	2,948,972	3,435,205
Government grants received	233,479	330,824
Intangible assets	1,624,244	1,442,344
Property, plant, and equipment	6,180,035	6,587,593
Total Assets	**36,138,791**	**44,295,341**
Liabilities		
Current liabilities	$ 985,988	2,187,193
Common Shares	42,462,206	42,465,000
Accumulated Deficit	(20,269,900)	(16,158,482)
Contributed Surplus	12,960,497	15,801,630
Total Liabilities and Shareholders' Equity	**36,138,791**	**44,295,341**

EXHIBIT V: SELECT FINANCIAL INFORMATION – STATEMENT OF OPERATIONS

GreenSmart Inc.

Statement of Operations

For the 3 Months Ended March 31, 2022 and 2023

	2023	2022
Sales	$ 4,910,436	5,757,462
Cost of sales	4,117,774	4,855,192.75
Expenses		
Selling, general, and administrative	3,311,672	3,429,152
Research and development	1,592,408	1,653,696.75
Loss from operations	−4,111,418	−4,180,579.5

FINANCIAL ACCOUNTING WITH FINANCE CONCEPTS CASE 3

RawHealth Inc.

RawHealth Inc. (RawHealth) is an importer and distributor of high-quality vegetables and mushrooms not grown or commonly available in Canada. When the vegetables arrive, they often need to be kept in special facilities to ripen fully and it can take up to four weeks before they are distributed to retailers. RawHealth distributes their products to mainly high-end retailers across the country. Many of RawHealth's partners are smaller stores serving a narrow target market (e.g., customers who prefer premium organic vegetables or who enjoy making exquisite authentic meals at home out of exotic ingredients). RawHealth has seen significant growth in revenue and profits over the past four years. Their executive team forecasts continued growth in both Canadian and US markets.

Due to this anticipated growth, RawHealth is considering purchasing a competitor. To finance the purchase, they have borrowed $5,000,000 from a private investor, who is a well-off relative of one of the company's founders.

The investor has placed a stipulation stating that if RawHealth's net income falls below $1,000,000 per year, the loan will become payable immediately (though the investor indicated that he might be a bit lenient on the repayment deadlines depending on the circumstances). Otherwise, RawHealth will repay the loan on January 1, 2028, while making an annual payment of 7% on the principal on January 1 of each year. The investor also requested the annual audited financial statements, starting the year ending December 31, 2022, which will be the first time RawHealth has been audited.

You, CPA, are a senior consultant at Calente LLP and have been engaged by RawHealth to advise on the accounting policies used for fiscal 2022 among other matters. The company's annual revenue is $6,000,000 and it follows accounting standards suitable for public enterprises. Based on the draft financial statements prepared by management, net income is currently $1,230,060 before tax and $890,000 after tax. Today is February 9, 2023.

RawHealth's CFO resigned during the 2022 financial year to spend more time with friends and family. When asked about the resignation, the CFO said, "I just couldn't do it anymore. I carried way too much responsibility. From approving transactions to reconciling bank statements and signing cheques, everything fell onto my plate. I needed a break."

Due to a change in regulations at the end of December 2022, RawHealth is being forced to discontinue equipment that is no longer considered compliant with government regulations by the beginning of 2024. They must also purchase new and compliant replacement equipment. The equipment to be sold was purchased on January 2, 2018, for $4,500,000 and was originally expected to last 15 years at which point it would have no residual value. The equipment accounts for approximately half of the company's annual revenues. Due to an order backlog that a compliant supplier, ComplianceEmporium (CE), is experiencing, RawHealth will have to wait two months to receive new equipment at a cost of $6,500,000. The Production and Sourcing team lead negotiated a special purchase order with RawHealth's existing supplier, outlined in Exhibit I, that can be delivered within one week.

Due to RawHealth's fast expansion, they had to purchase additional fridges for $600,000 at the beginning of July 2022. These fridges are expected to have a useful life of 20 years due to the significant wear and tear industrial fridges tend to undergo. RawHealth purchases product and materials used in operations from all over the world. Recently, due to the fluctuations in foreign currencies, RawHealth's management mentioned that managing currency risk has become more difficult.

In 2021, a RawHealth employee fell inside the plant. The employee launched a lawsuit against the company at the end of 2021. At that point in time, the company felt the lawsuit was frivolous and that the former employee would be sure to lose, and they didn't give it much thought. However, in 2022, upon further investigation, their lawyer said that it might be probable that the employee would win his claim and the company would have to pay approximately $500,000 in equal installments (i.e., $100,000 annually) over the next five years to compensate the employee for missed work.

On December 1, 2022, RawHealth launched a new "reward" system for their major customers as an attempt to provide volume discounts using a points system, where every kilogram of vegetables purchased earns a retailer one "point." If 1,000 points are collected within three months, the retailer will receive a 5% discount on their next order. If insufficient points are accumulated within three months, no discount is provided, the points balance becomes zero, and customers can start accumulating points for the next three months. No liability is currently recorded on the financial statements.

Prior to resigning, the CFO mentioned that RawHealth had no "real" system for tracking and logging loyalty points for their customers. This is mainly due to the fact that this type of system can be very costly and RawHealth prefers to spend excess cash on equipment to be used in production. The CFO admitted that RawHealth currently only keeps track of points for those clients that are believed to reach the bonus threshold. An Excel spreadsheet is used to track points for those clients. The rest of the points are not tracked.

EXHIBIT I: CONTRACT NEGOTIATED BY THE PRODUCTION AND SOURCING TEAM LEAD WITH EVERYTHING4U (E4U)

Everything4U sells equipment, machinery, kitchen appliances, and office supplies. Since the regulation change was made recently, E4U has not had the chance to overhaul their product offerings to meet the new standards. As a result, they have been offering special discounts and packages on affected products. The regular purchase price of equipment is $5,700,000. If RawHealth agrees to purchase fridges from E4U for $500,000, the price of equipment will be reduced to $5,000,000.

To purchase fridges from E4U, RawHealth would have to sell the new fridges purchased in July 2022. Since these fridges are only a few months old, RawHealth's Production and Sourcing team believes that there is a 60% chance they can be sold for $550,000, a 25% chance they can be sold for $490,000, and a 15% chance they can be sold for $450,000.

The Production and Sourcing team lead also negotiated with an equipment-refurbishing technician he was referred to by a close personal friend to make the equipment compliant with the new December 2022 regulations. The cost breakdown is estimated as follows:

Activity	Cost
Labour	$100,000
Disassembly	$200,000
Parts	$300,000
Miscellaneous	$150,000

RawHealth's annual revenue in 2022 was $20,400,000. It is expected to grow by 20% in 2023.

It is expected that the equipment will require continuous improvements for the first five years until regulations are solidified. The equipment from E4U will require $200,000 in the first year, $150,000 in the second year, and $75,000 for the remaining three years. The equipment from CE will require a $120,000 improvement for the first three years after which only ad hoc improvements will be required, estimated at $20,000.

As of today, RawHealth has not signed this contract because they cannot internally decide what is the best option for the company. It is important that they decide whether to purchase the equipment from Everything4U or from ComplianceEmporium as soon as possible. To this end, they have retained advisory services from the consulting division of Calente LLP to help them evaluate these options. Please add this analysis from an independent member of the consulting team and advise RawHealth.

EXHIBIT II: SELECT FINANCIAL INFORMATION OF RAWHEALTH AND MARKET DATA (FY22)

2018 bank loan: $20,000,000 per annum interest of 6%.

2020 loan from family friend of former CFO: $5,000,000 per annum interest of 7%.

Equity: $ 33,000,000.

Latest reported risk-free rate: 3.5%.

An investment firm recently conducted an analysis of the vegetable import and distribution market and determined that the systematic risk of the market is 1.21.

The equity risk premium was last assessed at 5%, however, this is expected to continue rising as the economy experiences rising interest rates.

RawHealth's corporate tax rate is 30%.

PART SEVEN

Financial Accounting with Tax Concepts Cases

FINANCIAL ACCOUNTING WITH TAX CONCEPTS CASE 1

Great Gifts Inc.

Melissa Kepper founded the gift basket company Great Gifts Inc. (GGI) five years ago. Melissa has been the driving force behind the growing business by catering to busy moms. Currently, GGI has become one of the leaders in this highly competitive market, offering a wide selection of premium gift baskets at prices below its competitors. GGI's baskets range from $100 to $200.

While Melissa has enjoyed running the business, her husband was recently promoted to a major executive position and is relocating to Australia. Melissa did not think it was possible to continue running the business and decided to sell it. Susan St. James, a potential buyer, requested that GGI's statements be audited. The company's books have never been audited, so to facilitate a possible sale, Melissa was fine with having the financial statements audited as per Susan's request. Melissa approached Michaela Pelligrino, who runs a smaller audit firm. Michaela's and Melissa's daughters go to the same school and have become good friends.

You, CPA, work for Pelligrino LLP, the firm hired to do the audit. In preparation for this year's audit, the partner has asked for you to complete an analysis of financial accounting issues and procedures on the accounting policies used for fiscal 2023. Melissa's part-time bookkeeper, Nina, says that GGI follows accounting standards required for private companies. Melissa has no accounting knowledge and relies on Nina for everything accounting related. Nina, who doesn't have an accounting background, has been bookkeeping for more than five years and gained most of her accounting knowledge from helping with the bookkeeping of her own family business. Today is February 1, 2024. The company's year-end is December 31. Susan is considering obtaining a personal line of credit from a bank to grow the business if she does purchase it. The borrowing rate for the loan would be 10%. Further, Melissa has requested that we identify any preliminary tax issues that may arise as part of the sale and her departure from Canada.

The purchase price, which is being discussed by both Susan and Melissa, is expected to be based on multiple of five times the average net income for the past two years. GGI's preliminary financial statements are reporting a 2023 and 2022 net income of $387,650 and $598,660, respectively.

GGI prides itself on its great selection of gift baskets. Melissa regularly toured North America and Europe to establish strong supplier relationships. Various types of goods are used in GGI baskets: herbal teas from the German Alps, essential oils from Spain, leather products from Italy, and Canadian maple syrup. Melissa admits that getting certain goods has been a challenge given all the supply shortages impacting many industries.

The price of goods can drastically fluctuate. In addition, GGI has to pay freight charges, which are usually about 5% of the purchase price, and taxes (paid in the country of purchase), which are about 10–15% of the purchase price. GGI often purchases inventory in bulk and rents a small storage facility for $400 per month. Sometimes products arrive slightly damaged and have to be thrown out. Upon arrival at GGI facilities, goods are assembled into baskets by the packaging department's five staff members. When it is busy (e.g., around Valentine's Day or holidays), Melissa herself spends the entire workday in the department to help assemble baskets. Currently all inventory costs are expensed as incurred, except for the direct purchase cost.

Staff members in the packaging department operate on a clock-in clock-out system. Melissa noticed that during slow times the labour hours are practically identical to holiday season hours and is unsure why. Timesheets are usually submitted to the bookkeeper and salaries are paid based on the timesheets submitted by employees.

GGI operates out of a leased office space, which includes several offices for admin staff and a medium-sized warehouse where goods are stored and all the packaging takes place. The office, situated in a 40-year-old industrial plaza, was leased out three years ago when GGI outgrew Melissa's basement. At that time, the lease agreement was signed for seven years. Monthly lease payments are $8,000. The contract stipulated that if either GGI or the landlord terminated the agreement early, a penalty of $50,000 would be paid to the other party. The landlord recently informed Melissa that they received an attractive offer from a developer who wanted to purchase several adjacent plazas to build a large office building. GGI has to move out by December 31, 2024. When Melissa priced out the office space rented out by GGI for purchase three years ago, it cost $165,000. The landlord tells her that the same space could now be sold for $200,000. These events are not reflected on GGI's financials, but Nina decreases cash by $8,000 and increases the operating expense by the same amount when making the monthly lease payment. At the time of signing the lease, the remaining useful life of the plaza is only 10 years.

In addition to the leased office space, Melissa and her husband owned a house and a cottage that they both ordinarily inhabited throughout their years of ownership. The house was purchased in 2013 and the cottage in 2018. As part of their departure from the country, both properties were sold in 2023. The capital gain on the house was $475,000 and the capital gain on the cottage was $347,000. Further, Melissa was wondering if there are any other potential tax implications when becoming a non-resident of the home country.

Even though GGI has always been focused on customer service, a new policy was established this fiscal year: if an order is incorrect or is delivered to the wrong address, GGI issues a $50 gift card to the customer redeemable towards their next purchase. The gift cards have no expiration date. Melissa says that none of the approximately 100 cards so far issued to customers have been redeemed. Nina did not make any journal entry in relation to the issuance of gift cards

As part of the gift card process, Melissa mentions that when a customer indicates that an order was incorrect, the validity of their claim is not checked in the system. Melissa mentions, "I simply do not have the time to see whether an order was correct or incorrect, besides, all of my customers can be trusted!"

Melissa also established a call center when she realized that clients might need help picking out gifts for custom baskets. She found that most gift basket websites do not offer the option of speaking to a live agent. Melissa hired 10 agents to work on a rotational basis at the call center. For every sale that an agent makes, they receive 3% commission of the sale's price. The commissions are paid on a quarterly basis, every March 1, June 1, September 1, and December 1. Nina increases bonus expense and decreases cash when the commissions are paid.

"I think you'll be able to expand GGI to operate nationally and eventually franchise it," Melissa told Susan. "That was my long-term plan. 'Great Gifts' is trademarked, so you can safely grow brand recognition. GGI paid $15,000 in legal and admin fees to register the trademark. However, I believe the business has established substantial goodwill with its customers, and if the Great Gifts name is sold, you could get at least $150,000 for it." You looked through the financials and found no account reflecting the trademark.

Melissa admits that the business is cyclical depending on the economic environment. Moreover, she has noticed a slight year-over-year decrease in sales recently. To counter the decrease, Melissa came up with a new way of generating revenue. Customers can now subscribe to a monthly delivery service. For example, if a customer wanted to send a pleasant surprise every month to an elderly parent, GGI will customize a monthly basket based on the customer's request. Customers can choose from either 6- or 12-month options and pay the full amount when signing up for the service. Melissa spent a lot of time advertising the service and it has been a big success. Nina records all payments when they are received.

To increase short-term cash flow, Melissa decided to sell one of GGI's depreciable capital assets. The proceeds of disposition were $37,500 and the undepreciated capital cost of the capital asset was $17,500. The asset was originally purchased in 2020 for $57,400 and was used actively in the day-to-day operations. Melissa mentioned how there should be no tax triggered on the disposition, as the asset was sold for less than its original cost.

FINANCIAL ACCOUNTING WITH TAX CONCEPTS CASE 2

Holistay Inc.

Holistay Inc. (HI) is a new Canadian-controlled private corporation that helps Canadians find a perfect place to vacation in their own province instead of going on holidays abroad. HI was founded in 2010 by Jethro and Hannah Butler, both Canadian residents and a husband and wife team. Jethro, a talented programmer, built a website that allows property owners to advertise and rent out their cottages to visitors for short-term stays. HI's main competitor is Airbnb. However, HI's revenue has been increasing each year and it holds a strong market position throughout the country and especially the region.

You, CPA, have been hired by HI in the role of a controller. Your primary duties are to advise on the preparation of the financial statements, establish appropriate accounting policies, and advise on any taxation issues that may arise. HI's statements will be audited at the end of the fiscal year by an independent auditor to ensure compliance with accounting standards. Given HI's growth, several potential investors have asked about investing in the business and want to review the audited financial statements once they are prepared. The year-end is November 30 and today is December 16. The Butlers have asked you to prepare a report on the recommended treatment of significant accounting and taxation issues. HI does not have any debt outstanding but if they needed to get a loan from the bank, the borrowing rate would be 7.5%.

COTTAGE RENTALS

When a cottage is rented using the HI website, HI keeps 40% of the total rental fee as commission and the rest of the fee is wired to the cottage owner. This is done automatically when the booking is made. All bookings are non-refundable.

A cottage was rented on November 20 for four days starting November 30. Afterwards, the cottage owner called HI very angry, saying that his cottage was "destroyed by out of control teenagers." He is looking for compensation from HI and to avoid bad publicity, HI will pay the owner $50,000 on December 20.

NEW SOFTWARE

In the beginning of the current fiscal year, Jethro decided that it was critical for HI to create a more sophisticated software system to remain competitive on the market. The new software had to make it even easier for visitors to use the website to search for properties that met their needs. Jethro, being busy with other aspects of the business, hired a team of programmers to build the software, and prepaid $120,000 for their work. However, after months of delay, it became evident that the team was not qualified to accomplish the task. Jethro fired the team, but they refused to return the money, arguing that Jethro did not give clear directions and that resulted in the project's failure. Jethro hired another team of more experienced programmers and stayed very involved with the project, spending approximately 25% of his total time on it. The new team was able to salvage a very minimal amount of the work done by the first team. Nevertheless, the new software was extremely successful the second time around and Jethro paid $150,000 to the second team after the project was completed. Jethro mentioned that sales grew by 15% since the launch of the new software.

NEW OPPORTUNITIES

The business has accumulated capital since it started, so the Butlers decided to expand their operations by investing in five premium lots in cottage country. They are building luxury cottages as rental properties, which will be featured on the HI website along with the other rental properties advertised there. After spending a lot of time and resources on the architectural design and décor, the cottages have managed to attract a lot of attention. HI receives many offers from affluent retirees asking to purchase the cottages. The Butlers simply could not pass on one offer, selling a new cottage at a premium price, and they are currently considering another offer. The Butlers are now planning to purchase several other lots. The profit made on the sale of the cottage was treated as a capital gain for tax purposes.

As the Butlers were designing the cottages, they paid particular attention to the kitchen areas, as that is where people tend to gather when hosting. Almost all of the fixtures (sinks, cabinets, etc.) were sourced from a company specializing in kitchens, BestWater Inc. (BWI). BWI was recently inherited by the founder's children, who learned when they inherited it that the company was on the verge of bankruptcy due to their father's frivolous spending. The Butlers really liked BWI's products and firmly believe that the company has great potential. Therefore, in the current fiscal year, HI purchased 18% of BWI's outstanding common shares, which injected some cash financing into BWI, allowing it to get back on track towards profitability. Currently, Jethro and Hannah also have two seats on its board of directors out of a total of four.

In the current fiscal year, HI sold its primary headquarters and moved into a brand new larger office five months later to meet the needs of its growing business. Since Hannah strongly believes that the real estate prices will only be increasing, she decided that it was necessary to purchase the office space as opposed to leasing it. The disposition of HI's old office space resulted in a capital gain of $275,050 and recapture of $125,070.

Jethro recently met one of the owners of a private company, MyDesign Inc., which runs a website that connects designers and clients. The website is free to visitors who want to explore various home designs but designers are charged a subscription fee to post their work. Given how similar this business model is to HI's (and he firmly believes this model is successful), Jethro thought it would be a good opportunity to purchase some shares. Luckily, one of the part-owners wanted to sell his 5% stake and thus, HI purchased 1,000 common shares, which constitutes 5% of all outstanding MyDesign shares. Jethro is not sure how long HI will be holding on to the shares (if the share price increases significantly or if the company goes public, Jethro will sell the shares at a profit) but he hopes that this investment will result not only in a quick profit but also potentially bring the two companies closer in a strategic way.

To quickly expand their operations, MyDesign had to obtain a large loan from a local bank. HI agreed to guarantee the bank loan that MyDesign was seeking at the beginning of the year. The bank requested quarterly financial statements to ensure they were meeting all of the covenants, including the current ratio covenant of 1:1. MyDesign's most recent financial statements indicate that the covenant was not met and the current ratio is 0.9:1. The company is now negotiating with the bank to waive the covenant for this quarter, as they are confident that they will meet it in the next quarter and onwards. If the negotiations fail, MyDesign will have to repay the loan immediately, but the company does not have the total amount available in cash. HI will thus have to pay some of the loan (since HI was a guarantor on the loan), but they are still unclear about the exact amount. The last Jethro heard, MyDesign's management told him that the negotiations were moving along well and that a bank representative said that it is probable that the covenants will be waived for this quarter, but the VP of lending's approval is still pending.

A MyDesign contractor approached Jethro to offer to help consult on website development and design. The arrangement would be on a contract basis, where Jethro would pay the individual $75/hour. The initial engagement would be for three months and the individual must submit a record of hours and invoice to HI every two weeks for the work completed. When negotiating the hourly rate, the contractor mentioned to Jethro that they have similar arrangements with other companies, but due to Jethro's connection with MyDesign, they accepted a cheaper rate.

FINANCIAL ACCOUNTING WITH TAX CONCEPTS CASE 3

Bleistift Inc.

Bleistift Inc. (BI) was started by Hans Berg 40 years ago. A German immigrant, Hans failed to find a job upon arrival but remembered his grandfather's passion for making hand-crafted pencils, and that's how Bleistift was founded (Bleistift means "pencil" in German). BI is a private corporation committed to creating and developing writing and drawing instruments using the finest materials. BI is known across the world among artists who use pencils for their artwork. Since BI primarily sells to artists, BI always experiences an increase in product demand when the economy is strong and people are willing to invest in artwork.

You, CPA, work at a public accounting firm that has just been appointed an auditor at BI. The company's year-end is September 30. BI follows accounting standards required for public enterprises. It is now October 27, 2023, and you are starting your preliminary work for the audit. As per the client's request, the audit must be completed by November 12, 2023. Hans, who is now 75, decided to retire but wants to give an equal share of the business to his three children, Berta, Helga, and Kaiser. To avoid any disagreements, the children decided to find an independent auditor to conduct a first-time audit on the financial statements to ensure that all accounting policies are appropriate. Further, the children have requested that a preliminary calculation be conducted on the income statement to estimate the taxable income for FY2023. As the children take over the business, they want to ensure that there is always enough cash on hand to pay the taxes owing, if any, each fiscal year. They have also requested that any other taxation issues and financial accounting issues be brought to their attention.

Berta has been involved in the business for the past 10 years, while Kaiser and Helga are not involved and do not plan to be as long as "Berta is doing a good job and I still get my dividends," as quipped by Kaiser. Berta told you that BI will require a bank loan in the future and has already begun the application process. When the bank loan is obtained, the interest rate of borrowing would be 4%. Berta feels the bank loan is required to provide a necessary "cushion" for the business in tough times, should economic conditions worsen further.

As part of the loan application, BI is required to disclose their preliminary financial statements for the FY2023 year-end. Due to rising prices of production and inflation, BI is currently showing an accounting net loss of $110,000 and gross profit of $375,000 (Exhibit). Both profits and gross margins have decreased year-over-year due to the current state of the economy.

Graphite, wood, and glue are the major components required for pencil manufacturing. All inventory, raw materials, work-in-progress, and finished goods are valued using the first-in, first-out method. An inventory count has never been conducted in the past, as Berta mentioned "our father always new exactly the amount of goods BI had on hand at any given time." All revenue is recognized when goods are shipped, except for an order from PicaSaw Inc.

Berta mentions to you that ever since Hans recently stepped down, there have been some inventory items missing compared to what BI has on record. Berta says, "I don't understand where some of our inventory goes. We store all product in a secure location that must be accessed by a key card that I keep in the lunchroom. Maybe the missing inventory has to do with my lack of accounting knowledge, and I'm not reconciling the books properly?"

BI currently has one bookkeeper on staff who works part-time three days a week. The bookkeeper, who has been with BI for over 25 years, indicated that once Hans fully retires, they will also step down from their role as Hans "practically did everything around here." From reconciling the bank to signing cheques, Hans ensured that every process and transaction went through him before being finalized.

In the beginning of the year, BI received a custom order to produce pencils for a wealthy family in Germany whose children are into drawing. The family ordered four custom sets with their children's names engraved on each pencil with small diamonds embedded at the top. Since the family was very pleased with the products, they recommended BI to their friends and suddenly BI found itself in a new line of business—custom-made pencils for wealthy

European families. Each set takes a couple of days to complete and only one set can be completed at one time (as special equipment is required and only one employee is responsible for this because of his extensive experience and skills). Often families order up to 10 sets in one order, which means they must wait a couple weeks after production begins before the completed package of goods can be sent to them.

In December 2022, BI purchased new equipment looking to expand their business. Unfortunately, the Canadian economy has been in a recessionary-like environment lately that has resulted in a business slowdown. BI stopped running its old equipment, which is more expensive to maintain, and is solely using its new equipment at present. BI has considered selling the old equipment for $1,000,000 all together but Berta has a hard time letting go of the equipment, as she is still hopeful that the business will pick up. If it does, Berta believes the equipment can run for another five years generating $200,000 each year. The equipment's current net book value is $1,200,000.

Just a couple of weeks ago, BI purchased some assets off a company that was exiting its paper-making business line. Berta could not resist a great purchase price of $800,000 for a complete set of manufacturing equipment, one-month worth of inventory required for production, and a patent. However, she admits that it was really the patent that most interested her. Berta says that the equipment would cost $500,000–$600,000 alone if purchased separately and she estimates that one-month worth of inventory would cost between $200,000–$300,000.

To keep employees happy and retain top talent, BI's management strongly believes in staff parties as well as giving top performers gifts and rewards for hard work. Every quarter, BI hosts a staff party where food and drinks are provided. As a component of the party, BI recognizes top performers and presents them with gifts. Gifts are given instead of cash bonuses, as BI believes that employees should not have to pay tax on rewards for their great service.

BI sells directly to consumers via its website and high-end specialty retail stores. One of BI's main partners is PicaSaw Inc., which is primarily located in Europe. In April 2023, PicaSaw was bought by a new investor who established new management and fully revised the company's growth plan. PicaSaw entered a heavy expansion phase and placed a large order of BI pencils. They were supposed to take delivery of these products on October 1, 2023. The expansion has not been going as well as hoped and PicaSaw asked BI to hold on to the products until they built enough locations to be able to store the inventory. PicaSaw did not give a specific point in time when they expected this to happen. All related revenue was recognized when the goods were set aside for shipment.

In December 2022, BI committed to sponsoring a graduation in a remote area high school that has a large population of children from single families. Due to expansion efforts, BI needed the cash when it came time to fund the event and pulled its sponsorship. At that time, the school had already planned a big gala, taking into consideration the extra funds that were supposed to be covered by BI. The school now had to cover the costs of the event out of its budget. The school administration filed a lawsuit against BI claiming that BI must compensate the school for the event. BI's lawyer states that "There is no reason why BI should be legally responsible for the event, however, BI should consider any implications on its reputation related to the event." This incident has not been reflected on BI's financial statements.

EXHIBIT: STATEMENT OF INCOME

Bleistift Inc.

Statement of Income

For the Year Ended September 30, 2023

Revenues - Note 1		$ 1,809,000
Cost of goods sold		1,434,000
Gross profit		375,000
Expenses		
Advertising **- Note 2**		$ 75,050
Vehicle and travel		23,270
Meals and entertainment		5,670
Insurance **- Note 3**		42,560
Subcontractors		13,450
Salaries and benefits **- Note 4**		190,500
Utilities		17,500
Occupancy costs		70,500
Depreciation **- Note 5**		35,000
Provision for income taxes		11,500
Net Loss		**−110,000**

Note 1 - Includes a gain of $34,000 on sale of capital asset.
Note 2 - $33,400 pertains to foreign advertising aimed at the Canadian market.
Note 3 - Life insurance premiums were $23,000. Premiums were paid on a non-group policy and was not part of collateral for a loan.
Note 4 - $75,800 pertains to an accrued bonus to be paid June 15, 2024.
Note 5 - Capital Cost Allowance for the year, which includes immediate expensing, was $55,600.

FSC
www.fsc.org
MIX
Papier | Fördert gute Waldnutzung
FSC® C083411

Kolibri 360 GmbH
Ferdinand-Jühlke-Straße 7
99095 Erfurt, Deutschland
produktsicherheit@kolibri360.de